BUILDING A CIVILIZATION OF LOVE

Deacon Harold Burke-Sivers

Building a Civilization of Love

A Catholic Response to Racism

IGNATIUS PRESS   SAN FRANCISCO

Nihil Obstat: Mr. Todd Cooper, M.A., S.T.B.
          Censor Librorum

Imprimatur: + The Most Reverend Alexander K. Sample,
          J.C.L.
          Archbishop of Portland, Oregon
          August 1, 2023

Cover image:
Right panel of an Ethiopian Orthodox icon triptych,
circa late 17th-early 18th century.
From the collection of the National Museum of African Art,
Smithsonian Institution, Washington, D.C.

Cover design by John Herreid

© 2023 by Ignatius Press, San Francisco
All rights reserved
ISBN 978-1-62164-546-7 (PB)
ISBN 978-1-64229-197-1 (eBook)
Library of Congress Catalogue Number 2023933668
Printed in the United States of America ∞

For people of goodwill everywhere who
have given their lives in the peaceful pursuit
of racial justice and equality

CONTENTS

INTRODUCTION

There is no true love without an awareness that God "is
Love"—and that man is the only creature on earth which
God has called into existence "for its own sake". Created
in the image and likeness of God, man cannot fully "find
himself" except through the sincere gift of self. Without
such a concept of man, of the person and the "communion of persons" in the family, there can be no civilization of love; similarly, without the civilization of love it is
impossible to have *such a concept of person and of the communion of persons.*

—Pope John Paul II, *Letter to Families,*
no. 13; emphasis in original

This book, inspired by the above quote from Pope Saint
John Paul II, is about a Catholic—not a secular or worldly—
response to the epidemic of racism. Do not expect to see
economic, political, or sociological solutions. Instead, my
approach will be firmly rooted in the Scriptures, the natural law, and the teachings of the Catholic Church.

The initial chapter sets the stage for what follows. In it,
I will define racism and make a clear distinction between
"racism" and "prejudice". These terms have become conflated within the culture and need to be distinguished so
that a clear understanding of what racism is and is not can
be established.

I will then explore the Sacred Scriptures to see what
they have to tell us about the connection between racism

and the institutional practice of "slavery", which was a multidimensional concept that included various forms of servitude including chattel slavery.

In the second chapter, I will examine the Church's historical response to racism, particularly the attitudes and practices of the Church in the United States, and provide evidence of magisterial teaching in the form of papal and conciliar pronouncements on racism and slavery throughout the last two millennia.

The following three chapters will look at ideologies that are being incorporated into some corners of the Church as ways supposedly to help Catholics better understand the issue of race. These include critical race theory, liberation theology, and the Black Lives Matter movement, respectively.

I approach all three subjects objectively and with an open mind, asking the same question for each discipline: Is there anything contained within these approaches that Catholics can utilize to facilitate the healing and reconciliation of racial division? After reading the source documentation written by proponents of each method I determined that, from a Catholic perspective focused specifically on responding to the evil of racism, none of these concepts are very helpful and, in point of fact, may even exacerbate and widen the racial divide.

The last chapter articulates a grassroots, parish-based strategy that I consider to be a truly Catholic response to racism. Ameliorating racism is not a Band-Aid fix. It is going to require a lot of hard work, dedication, and sacrifice. It means that we must become vulnerable and, in doing so, we will become acutely aware of our personal weaknesses.

But we are not without hope! After the Lord revealed to Saint Paul that "my grace is sufficient for you, for my power is made perfect in weakness," Paul writes, "I will all the more gladly boast of my weaknesses, that the power of Christ may rest upon me. For the sake of Christ, then, I am content with weaknesses, insults, hardships, persecutions, and calamities; for when I am weak, then I am strong."[1]

My approach may seem overly optimistic to some but is squarely rooted in biblical principles, particularly in seeing the image and likeness of God in every person as the foundation for change.[2] I am also keenly aware that the task of remedying racial injustice is a participation in the redemptive work of Christ, and that the courage we must summon to meet this challenge head-on reflects a "work of faith and labor of love and steadfastness of hope in our Lord Jesus Christ".[3]

Once we start to see people the way God sees them, we will begin to appreciate the culturally diverse gifts each person brings to the life of the Church. This, in turn, will lead to a greater promotion of honest conversation and dialogue that, of course, must be grounded in a deep and meaningful life of prayer.

A couple of other observations should be noted. I deliberately avoid using the insulting term "minority" to describe non-Caucasian persons. Rather, throughout the book, I refer to our brothers and sisters as "people of color", which is a better and more accurate descriptor. I also do not use popular jargon like "African American" as these terms have a tendency to exclude (although not deliberately) people who do not fit into these socially constructed categories.

Ultimately, this book is for all races and ethnicities, yet I am cognizant of the fact that I am writing from the perspective and experience of a black Catholic. I desire everyone

[1] 2 Cor 12:9–10.
[2] Cf. Gen 1:26–27.
[3] 1 Thess 1:3.

to see himself and his story in these pages. I sincerely hope that this book will be used as a starting point for deeper introspection about race-related issues, allowing love to alleviate fear so that the difficult questions surrounding racism may be asked in an environment that does not deny the inherent dignity of the human person but paves a pathway forward in true justice and peace where, transformed by the Sacred Heart of Jesus, we become vehicles of divine mercy in the lives of others.

My prayer is that Catholics become more confident and motivated to take the lead in addressing racial inequality both within the Church and in the greater society. As Pope Saint Clement I states in his *Letter to the Corinthians*, this can come about "if our understanding be fixed by faith towards God; if we earnestly seek the things which are pleasing and acceptable to Him; if we do the things which are in harmony with His blameless will; and if we follow the way of truth, casting away from us all unrighteousness and iniquity, along with all covetousness, strife, evil practices, deceit, whispering, and evil-speaking."[4] With the help of God's grace, let us not be afraid to pick up this cross and follow Christ so that His great desire for unity among His people may be fulfilled: "The glory which you have given me I have given to them, that they may be one even as we are one, I in them and you in me, that they may become perfectly one, so that the world may know that you have sent me and have loved them even as you have loved me."[5]

---

[4] Pope Clement I, *Letter to the Corinthians* 35, trans. John Keith, in *Ante-Nicene Fathers*, vol. 9, ed. Allan Menzies (Buffalo, N.Y.: Christian Literature Publishing, 1896). Revised and edited for New Advent by Kevin Knight, http://www.newadvent.org/fathers/1010.htm.

[5] Jn 17:22–23.

CHAPTER ONE

Prejudice and Racism

The Reverend Dr. Martin Luther King, Jr., spoke the following eloquent words when he accepted the Nobel Peace Prize: "Sooner or later all the people of the world will have to discover a way to live together in peace, and thereby transform this pending cosmic elegy into a creative psalm of brotherhood."[1] He went on to say that if peace and racial equality are to be achieved, "man must evolve for all human conflict a method which rejects revenge, aggression and retaliation. The foundation of such a method is love."[2] Dr. King is speaking of a love rooted in faith, a faith that acknowledges that "God is love, and he who abides in love abides in God, and God abides in him."[3]

Loving as God loves means that human love must be a free choice of the will; we must use our personal freedom to choose to love God before and above all else. Loving as God loves means that the dignity and value of every person must be preserved, keeping in mind that all of God's children are made in His image and likeness. Loving as God loves means that our love must be

---

[1] Martin Luther King, Jr., "Acceptance Speech" (University of Oslo, Oslo, Norway, December 10, 1964), NobelPrize.org, https://www.nobelprize.org/prizes/peace/1964/king/acceptance-speech/.

[2] Ibid.

[3] 1 Jn 4:16.

a self-gift: we must surrender ourselves in love for the sake of others and so enter more deeply into the life of Christ. Loving as God loves means that our love must be permanent because God will not accept anything less than our total, complete, and lifelong commitment to serving Him. Racial injustice and prejudice are not only antithetical to loving as God loves but are also affronts to truth, freedom, and peace.

In order to address adequately issues of race from a Catholic perspective, it is important to define our terms. "Race" is a complex word with multifaceted layers of meaning. *Merriam-Webster* lists three distinct definitions of "race", all of which have several subdefinitions. The primary meaning of race states that "race" is "any one of the groups that humans are often divided into based on physical traits regarded as common among people of shared ancestry."[4] "Race" can also mean

the fact of dividing people, or of people being divided, into such groups: categorization by race ...

a group of people sharing a common cultural, geographical, linguistic, or religious origin or background ...

the descendants of a common ancestor: a group sharing a common lineage.[5]

The following pericope from the Book of Numbers will help illustrate the intricacies surrounding the issue of race.

Miriam and Aaron spoke against Moses because of the Cushite [Ethiopian] woman whom he had married, for

[4] *Merriam-Webster Online*, s.v. "race (*n.*)", accessed December 8, 2022, https://www.merriam-webster.com/dictionary/race.

[5] Ibid.

he had married a Cushite woman.... And the anger of the LORD was kindled against them, and he departed; and when the cloud removed from over the tent, behold, *Miriam was leprous, as white as snow.* And Aaron turned towards Miriam, and behold, she was leprous. And Aaron said to Moses, "Oh, my lord, *do not punish us because we have done foolishly and have sinned.*"[6]

Miriam, Aaron, and Moses are Israelites, of whom God said, "You shall be my people, and I will be your God."[7] The nation of Israel shared a common cultural, geographical, linguistic, and religious origin rooted in covenant relationship with YHWH (Yahweh). Israel was considered God's chosen race through whom the other races would come to know and serve the one true God. God told Ezekiel, "I will make a covenant of peace with them; it shall be an everlasting covenant with them; and I will bless them and multiply them, and will set my sanctuary in the midst of them for evermore. My dwelling place shall be with them; and I will be their God, and they shall be my people. Then the nations will know that I the LORD sanctify Israel, when my sanctuary is in the midst of them for evermore."[8]

Miriam and Aaron take issue with the fact that Moses married a woman outside of the Israelite race; their *principal* objection was not based on the color of her skin. This attitude stems from the fact that the people of Israel believed they were not to engage in interracial marriages. The

---

[6] Num 12:1, 9–11; my emphasis.

[7] Jer 30:22.

[8] Ezek 37:26–28. The idea of the "chosen people" would later apply to Christians as followers of Jesus Christ: "But you are a chosen race, a royal priesthood, a holy nation, God's own people, that you may declare the wonderful deeds of him who called you out of darkness into his marvelous light" (1 Pet 2:9).

Israelites were especially chosen and singled out by God for personal relationship. They enjoyed covenant intimacy with Him, something the other races did not have. In fact, the Israelites believed they were so enveloped with God's favor that they could subjugate the pagan nations that surrounded them:

> When the LORD your God brings you into the land which you are entering to take possession of it, and clears away many nations before you, the Hittites, the Girgashites, the Amorites, the Canaanites, the Perizzites, the Hivites, and the Jebusites, seven nations greater and mightier than yourselves, and when the LORD your God gives them over to you, and you defeat them; then you must utterly destroy them; you shall make no covenant with them, and show no mercy to them. You shall not make marriages with them, giving your daughters to their sons or taking their daughters for your sons.[9]

Moses' interracial marriage, then, was seen as an insult to Israelite culture. Moses had several wives, and it seemed unfair to Miriam and Aaron that his Cushite wife should enjoy the same privileges as his Israelite wives.[10] It is also reasonable to infer that Moses' decision led Miriam and

[9] Deut 7:1–3.

[10] Scripture nowhere presents polygamy and concubinage as part of God's design for creation or as morally licit. Far from being complicit in the practices of ancient cultures that harmed and oppressed women and children, both the Old and New Testaments rigidly uphold monogamy as normative. While it is true that Scripture records acts of polygamy and concubinage among Old Testament men, recording an action is not in itself a commendation of that action. God allowed this not as a direct commandment, but as a concession to help people to work toward His direct will, which is monogamy. The marriage pattern established at Creation—one man and one woman in a monogamous commitment—is both commanded and commended throughout the rest of Scripture. In our Lord's own words, "For your hardness of heart Moses allowed you to divorce your wives, but from the beginning it was not so" (Mt 19:8).

Aaron to question his authority and good judgment in leading the people.

God's response clearly vindicates Moses, a trusted servant to whom He revealed Himself. The Lord shows His displeasure with Miriam and Aaron's remarks by inflicting Miriam with a mild form of leprosy, turning her skin white (a striking juxtaposition to the dark skin of Moses' Ethiopian wife). Aaron, on his and Miriam's behalf, fully acknowledges their sin in questioning Moses' decision and appeals to Moses to intercede with God for Miriam's healing. They had forgotten God's words in the desert commanding them, "You shall not wrong a stranger or oppress him, for you were strangers in the land of Egypt";[11] and YHWH reminds Miriam and Aaron that racial injustice, whether cultural or physical, is not in accord with God's purposes and will not be tolerated.

What, then, is racism and how is it different from prejudice? This important distinction must be made since almost every negative race-related incident reported in the media is deemed "racist".

Prejudice with regard to race is a preconceived notion about someone because of race that is not based on adequate factual or objective experience, which often leads to stereotyping. Racism is prejudice or discrimination directed toward someone of a different race rooted in the belief that one race is superior to another.

For example, at a parish mission a few years ago, a white person discovered that I completed my undergraduate degree at the University of Notre Dame and said, "You went to Notre Dame? What position did you play?" Perhaps the calculus going on in his mind was something like this: an athletically built black man plus Notre Dame equals football. If so, then this individual's comment

[11] Ex 22:21.

was prejudiced and ignorant, since it was based solely on my physical appearance. But it would not necessarily have been racist. In order for his statement to be racist, his attitude behind the question or motive for asking it would have reflected the ludicrous belief that black people are not intelligent enough to be accepted academically into a school of that caliber, so the only way a person of color could be admitted was on athletic scholarship. This was not the case, as I saw from his embarrassed reaction upon learning that I had received an academic scholarship. The question he should have asked was, "You went to Notre Dame? What did you study?" because that is what he would have asked anyone else.

Obviously, we all have prejudices—maybe even racially biased prejudices—and may make unreflective presuppositions. Sometimes these are based on little more than generalizations due to limited experience or hearsay that often readily give way to simple encounters or experiences that call our attention to their inadequacies and inappropriateness, as clearly indicated by the above example.

Nevertheless, some people will want to label the above incident as an example of "racism", but that response itself is what I would call "emotional racism"—that is, having a negative emotional reaction to what, on the surface, *appears* to be racism but is actually an experience of prejudice. In short, "emotional racism" posits that every negative interaction or misunderstanding between people of different colors can be blamed on racism.

The incident with Miriam and Aaron against Moses is an example of racism since their comments were clearly intended to denote the superiority of Israel over other races. Likewise, individuals and organizations that promote supremacy of one race over another are rightly characterized as racist.

All of us, to some extent, harbor some level of prejudice. If I am speaking to people from the South, for example, I tend to assume they like to eat shrimp and grits. This assumption is not based in fact—not all Southerners by definition or by universal behavior like to eat shrimp and grits. It is a presupposition I tend to hold the evidence for which is simply anecdotal on my part. Since I know many Southerners who enjoy shrimp and grits, my attitude inclines me to suppose that if you are a Southern, you like shrimp and grits.

Both prejudices and racism are learned outlooks and behaviors. We consume images and sound bites from television, movies, and social media. We are influenced by family members and friends. We are inundated with examples, stereotypes, and caricatures of various races that are often belittling and derisive and, even if only subliminally, plant seeds of half-truths in the minds and hearts of the viewer or listener, or of family and friends. When you see, for example, images of people of color as slaves, domestics, and gang members day after day and year after year, or are exposed to a steady stream of racial jokes and slurs from peers, these portrayals work their way into our psyche and unintentionally can become, to some extent, "true" or "the way it is" in our thinking.

Prejudiced and racist attitudes of individuals also infiltrate institutional structures and organizations, thus forming the foundation for systemic racism. Slavery, the *Dred Scott v. John F. Sanford* Supreme Court decision, Jim Crow laws, apartheid, the Tuskegee Syphilis Study, and redlining are clear examples of this. Even in the history of the Church, Catholic leaders and organizations chose to follow civil law rather than the law of God by owning slaves, implementing segregation in the churches, and excluding people of color from full and equal participation in the life of the Church. The residual effects of these attitudes are still felt by many Catholics today.

At Immaculate Heart of Mary parish in Portland, Oregon, where I serve as deacon, many of the American black Catholic families immigrated to the Northwest from Louisiana and Alabama to work in the shipyards during World War II. Since the parish is close by, many families began attending Mass at the traditionally German and Irish parish. Today, they share their painful experiences of having to sit in the choir loft or in the back of the church, of not feeling welcomed as part of the Catholic family. Although the sting of these appalling practices has faded over time, the memories of the humiliation and shame still remain.

That said, we must be careful with the terms "institutional" racism and "systemic" racism. In order to claim factually that an institution is racist, you must show that it actively promotes through official or unofficial policies, procedures, directives, etc., the belief that one race is superior to another. Institutional racism must be distinguished from individuals within institutions who continue to hold prejudiced and racist attitudes.

Evangelical preacher and pastor Dr. Tony Evans gives a poignant example of institutional racism when he tells the history of the golf course owned by his congregation, Oak Cliff Bible Fellowship.

> The rule was black people could not play on the golf course. That was the rule. So we'll call that an unjust law. It then got turned over into membership ownership.... We don't have the law that blacks can't be members but we're going to set up a system that does not allow them to be members. So [this was] the system: before you could become a member, an existing member had to recommend you, but when the existing member recommended you, two-thirds of the membership had to vote for you.

So let's say an Anglo man has a great black friend; nothing about him is racist. He goes to the club and he says, "I want my African American friend to become a member of this club." He's got to do that up against the system, and that system says two-thirds of us have to agree with the way you feel. Until 1994, no black would be voted in because of the system, not because there was this law; it was this system that came from a law. Let's say you are Anglo and you're part of the one-third that voted to let him in, well, you still lost because the two-thirds did not vote that way. You could come out and argue, "But I am not one of those people. I am not a racist," and you could be absolutely right. But the system that you are a part of is and because you're part of that system, you get swept up even though you're not a personal racist and even though you voted the other way because the system didn't allow your nonracist perspective to win.[12]

We have to make a distinction between institutional racism and racist individuals within institutions. The United States government is no longer racist (there are very strict antidiscrimination and civil rights laws now in place), but there are, no doubt, individuals within the government who exhibit prejudice, are blatantly racist, or desire to perpetuate obsolete racist structures. For example, you may have an elected official who does not want people of color on his staff because he believes they are not as intelligent as their white counterparts. It may also be the case that a government loan officer may deny loans to people of color, not due to their inability to repay the loan, but because he feels more comfortable granting loans to white people.

[12] "Kingdom Race Theology #1—Sermon by Dr. Tony Evans", Oak Cliff Bible Fellowship, July 14, 2021, video, 13:50–16:21, posted August 2, 2021, https://www.youtube.com/watch?v=ao7sNItCkAY.

The Church herself, founded by Jesus Christ, is not racist (in fact, she cannot be racist), but there are undoubtedly individuals within the Church (both clergy and laity) who are racists. We must recognize the fact that we are all sinners in need of God's mercy, that we are still dealing with the effects of Original Sin, and that Christ calls us to transcend racist ideology and strive diligently for holiness. As the Second Vatican Council notes in the document *Lumen Gentium*,

> The Church ... is believed to be indefectibly holy. Indeed Christ, the Son of God, who with the Father and the Spirit is praised as "uniquely holy," loved the Church as His bride, delivering Himself up for her. He did this that He might sanctify her. He united her to Himself as His own body and brought it to perfection by the gift of the Holy Spirit for God's glory. Therefore in the Church, everyone whether belonging to the hierarchy, or being cared for by it, is called to holiness.[13]

The Bible and Biblical Response to Racism

The Scriptures are replete with examples of how we are to respond to racism, which is absolutely unacceptable because it goes against the mind of God.

We, as followers of Christ, are not to show prejudice or bias toward one person over another.

> LEVITICUS 19:15. You shall do no injustice in judgment; you shall not be partial to the poor or defer to the great, but in righteousness shall you judge your neighbor.

---

[13] Vatican Council II, Dogmatic Constitution on the Church *Lumen Gentium* (November 21, 1964), no. 39, https://www.vatican.va/archive/hist_councils /ii_vatican_council/documents/vat-ii_const_19641121_lumen-gentium_en .html.

DEUTERONOMY 1:17. You shall not be partial in judgment.

DEUTERONOMY 16:19. You shall not pervert justice; you shall not show partiality.

PROVERBS 24:23. These also are sayings of the wise. Partiality in judging is not good.

ACTS 10:34–35. And Peter opened his mouth and said: "Truly I perceive that God shows no partiality, but in every nation any one who fears him and does what is right is acceptable to him."

COLOSSIANS 3:25. For the wrongdoer will be paid back for the wrong he has done, and there is no partiality.

We, as servants of the King of Kings and the Lord of Lords, are not to judge people based on their outward appearance.

1 SAMUEL 16:7. But the LORD said to Samuel, "Do not look on his appearance or on the height of his stature, because I have rejected him; for the LORD sees not as man sees; man looks on the outward appearance, but the LORD looks on the heart."

JOHN 7:24. Do not judge by appearances, but judge with right judgment.

We, as disciples of Christ, are not to harbor hatred in our hearts toward others.

LEVITICUS 19:17–18. You shall not hate your brother in your heart, but you shall reason with your neighbor, lest you bear sin because of him. You shall not take vengeance or bear any grudge against the sons of your own people, but you shall love your neighbor as yourself: I am the LORD.

1 JOHN 2:11. But he who hates his brother is in the darkness and walks in the darkness, and does not know where he is going, because the darkness has blinded his eyes.

Instead, we are called to love others by seeing them through God's eyes by our faith and works.

MATTHEW 22:36–39. [A Pharisee asked Jesus,] "Teacher, which is the great commandment in the law?" And he said to him, "You shall love the Lord your God with all your heart, and with all your soul, and with all your mind. This is the great and first commandment. And a second is like it, You shall love your neighbor as yourself."

LUKE 6:27–28, 32–33, 35–37. Love your enemies, do good to those who hate you, bless those who curse you, pray for those who abuse you.... If you love those who love you, what credit is that to you? For even sinners love those who love them. And if you do good to those who do good to you, what credit is that to you? For even sinners do the same.... But love your enemies, and do good, and lend, expecting nothing in return; and your reward will be great, and you will be sons of the Most High; for he is kind to the ungrateful and the selfish. Be merciful, even as your Father is merciful. Judge not, and you will not be judged; condemn not, and you will not be condemned; forgive, and you will be forgiven.

JOHN 13:34–35. A new commandment I give to you, that you love one another; even as I have loved you, that you also love one another. By this all men will know that you are my disciples, if you have love for one another.

GALATIANS 3:28. There is neither Jew nor Greek, there is neither slave nor free, there is neither male nor female; for you are all one in Christ Jesus.

We are called by God to lay aside our differences and embrace peace, reconciliation, and unity as followers of Christ.

EPHESIANS 2:11–17, 19–22. Therefore remember that at one time you Gentiles in the flesh, called the uncircumcision by what is called the circumcision, which is made in the flesh by hands—remember that you were at that time separated from Christ, alienated from the commonwealth of Israel, and strangers to the covenants of promise, having no hope and without God in the world. But now in Christ Jesus you who once were far off have been brought near in the blood of Christ. For he is our peace, who has made us both one, and has broken down the dividing wall of hostility, by abolishing in his flesh the law of commandments and ordinances, that he might create in himself one new man in place of the two, so making peace, and might reconcile us both to God in one body through the cross, thereby bringing the hostility to an end. And he came and preached peace to you who were far off and peace to those who were near.... So then you are no longer strangers and sojourners, but you are fellow citizens with the saints and members of the household of God, built upon the foundation of the apostles and prophets, Christ Jesus himself being the cornerstone, in whom the whole structure is joined together and grows into a holy temple in the Lord; in whom you also are built into it for a dwelling place of God in the Spirit.

COLOSSIANS 3:11–15. Here there cannot be Greek and Jew, circumcised and uncircumcised, barbarian, Scythian, slave, free man [sic], but Christ is all, and in all. Put on then, as God's chosen ones, holy and beloved, compassion, kindness, lowliness, meekness, and patience, forbearing one another and, if one has a complaint against another, forgiving each other; as the Lord has forgiven you, so you also must forgive. And over all these put on love, which binds everything together in perfect harmony. And let the peace of Christ rule in your hearts, to which indeed you were called in the one body.

We are called to unity as one body—one race—in Christ, but there is an apparently glaring contradiction, which is the elephant in the room: Doesn't the Bible endorse racism by allowing the practice of slavery? In order to answer this question, we must have a correct understanding of what slavery is and how it was practiced in the ancient Near East.

The Bible and Slavery

I begin this section by identifying several types of slavery mentioned in the Bible. In doing so, I am not attempting to rationalize or endorse slavery in any way, shape, or form, but simply explaining biblical slavery in its literal-historical context.

Chattel Slavery

EXODUS 1:11, 13–14. Therefore they [the Egyptians] set taskmasters over them [the Israelites] to afflict them with heavy burdens.... They made the sons of Israel serve with rigor, and made their lives bitter with hard service, in mortar and brick, and in all kinds of work in the field; in all their work they made them serve with rigor.

Indentured Servitude

LEVITICUS 25:39–43. And if your brother becomes poor beside you, and sells himself to you, you shall not make him serve as a slave: he shall be with you as a hired servant and as a sojourner. He shall serve with you until the year of the jubilee; then he shall go out from you, he and his children with him, and go back to his own family, and return to the possession of his fathers. For they are my servants, whom I brought forth out of the land of Egypt; they shall not be sold as slaves. You shall not rule over him with harshness, but shall fear your God.

Conjugal Servitude

EXODUS 21:7–11. When a man sells his daughter as a slave, she shall not go out as the male slaves do. If she does not please her master, who has designated her for himself, then he shall let her be redeemed; he shall have no right to sell her to a foreign people, since he has dealt faithlessly with her. If he designates her for his son, he shall deal with her as with a daughter. If he takes another wife to himself, he shall not diminish her food, her clothing, or her marital rights. And if he does not do these three things for her, she shall go out for nothing, without payment of money.

Permanent Enslavement

EXODUS 21:2–6. When you buy a Hebrew slave, he shall serve six years, and in the seventh he shall go out free, for nothing. If he comes in single, he shall go out single; if he comes in married, then his wife shall go out with him. If his master gives him a wife and she bears him sons or daughters, the wife and her children shall be her master's and he shall go out alone. But if the slave plainly says, "I love my master, my wife, and my children; I will not go out free," then his master shall bring him to God, and he shall bring him to the door or the doorpost; and his master shall bore his ear through with an awl; and he shall serve him for life.

Penal Enslavement

LEVITICUS 25:44–46. As for your male and female slaves whom you may have: you may buy male and female slaves from among the nations that are round about you. You may also buy from among the strangers who sojourn with you and their families that are with you, who have been born in your land; and they may be your property. You may bequeath them to your sons after you, to inherit as a possession for ever; you may make slaves of them, but over your brethren the sons of Israel you shall not rule, one over another, with harshness.

These examples raise huge questions: If slavery was seen by God as unequivocally intolerable and contrary to His will, then why does God allow it? Why do the Israelites participate in the practice of slavery when they were slaves themselves?

It is important to note that the Israelites did not participate in chattel slavery where individuals were taken against their will and forced into servitude. In ancient Near Eastern culture, and for Israel, this was a crime punishable by death: "If a [man] has stolen the young son of a(nother) [man], he shall be put to death."[14]

The common practice of ancient Near Eastern cultures regarding slavery was indentured servitude where a distinction was made between native and foreign slaves. Native slaves were citizens who had fallen on hard times

---

[14]James B. Pritchard, ed., "Laws from Mesopotamia and Asia Minor (The Code of Hammurabi)", in *Ancient Near Eastern Texts Relating to the Old Testament* (Princeton, N.J.: Princeton University Press, 1969), 166. Biblical references include Exodus 21:16, "Whoever steals a man, whether he sells him or is found in possession of him, shall be put to death", and Deuteronomy 24:7, "If a man is found stealing one of his brethren, the sons of Israel, and if he treats him as a slave or sells him, then that thief shall die; so you shall purge the evil from the midst of you."

and willingly entered into slavery to pay off a debt, to compensate for stolen goods or survive a famine. For example, the Code of Hammurabi states that "if an obligation came due against a [man] and he sold (the services of) his wife, his son, or his daughter, or he has been bound over to service, they shall work (in) the house of their purchaser or obligee [sic] for three years, with their freedom being reestablished in the fourth year."[15] In this form of Israelite slavery, as articulated in the Book of Deuteronomy, once the debt was repaid, the person was released and given provisions to start a new life: "If your brother, a Hebrew man, or a Hebrew woman, is sold to you, he shall serve you six years, and in the seventh year you shall let him go free from you. And when you let him go free from you, you shall not let him go empty-handed; you shall furnish him liberally out of your flock, out of your threshing floor, and out of your wine press; as the LORD your God has blessed you, you shall give to him."[16]

There were also rules for Israelites who sold themselves to other nations (races) as slaves. Leviticus teaches that

> if a stranger or sojourner with you becomes rich, and your brother beside him becomes poor and sells himself to the stranger or sojourner with you, or to a member of the stranger's family, then after he is sold he may be redeemed; one of his brothers may redeem him, or his uncle, or his cousin may redeem him, or a near kinsman belonging to his family may redeem him; or if he grows rich he may redeem himself. He shall reckon with him who bought him from the year when he sold himself to him until the year of jubilee, and the price of his release shall be according to the number of years; the time he was with his

[15] Ibid., 170–71.
[16] Deut 15:12–14.

owner shall be rated as the time of a hired servant. If there
are still many years, according to them he shall refund out
of the price paid for him the price for his redemption. If
there remain but a few years until the year of jubilee, he
shall make a reckoning with him; according to the years
of service due from him he shall refund the money for
his redemption. As a servant hired year by year shall he
be with him; he shall not rule with harshness over him
in your sight. And if he is not redeemed by these means,
then he shall be released in the year of jubilee, he and his
children with him.[17]

Foreign slaves were people of other nations who were typically considered part of the spoils of war and subjected
to penal enslavement. According to Jewish scholar James
A. Diamond,

> The rabbis make no attempt to soften this. In fact, at least
> some voices in rabbinic literature interpret [Lev 25:46] not
> as permission to keep slaves forever but as a command-
> ment to do so. "... Rav Yehudah said: 'Whoever frees
> his slave has violated a positive commandment, as it says,
> "You shall work them forever."'"
>
> Nevertheless, the rabbis did take some small steps by
> codifying a prohibition against humiliating non-Israelite
> slaves. "... Samuel said: 'You shall work them forever—I
> gave them to you for work, but not for humiliation.'"[18]

The great rabbinic scholar Moses Maimonides (1138–
1205) in his *Laws on Slavery*, continues Diamond,

[17] Lev 25:47–54.

[18] James A. Diamond, "The Treatment of Non-Israelite Slaves: From Moses
to Moses", under "Non-Hebrew Slaves in the Bible", TheTorah.com, 2022,
https://www.thetorah.com/article/the-treatment-of-non-israelite-slaves
-from-moses-to-moses. The quote from Rav Yehudah is cited from b. *Berachot*
47b. The quote from Samuel is cited from b. *Niddah* 47a.

expresses moral discomfort with the idea, endorsed by the Torah, that an Israelite master *is* to work his non-Israelite slaves with harsh labor (*pharekh*), which he defines as ... "No defined limit is set for the work" [and] "Useless work." In both cases, the slave is not allowed a semblance of accomplishment that could salvage some sense of self-worth or empowerment as a human being. In effect, the master replaces God as the supreme object of the slave's obedience and dependence. Thus, this may account for why the classical rabbis considered keeping a slave past the obligatory sabbatical limit tantamount to idolatry.[19]

However, later Rabbinic scholars, including Maimonides, would soften the interpretation of the teaching on non-Israelite slaves. Diamond continues, "Focusing on the imposition of *pharekh* labor, Maimonides writes [that it is] best to be compassionate and not overburden slaves: 'It is permissible to have a Canaanite slave perform excruciating labor (*pharekh*). Although this is the law, the attribute of piety and the ways of wisdom is for a person to be compassionate and to pursue justice, not to excessively burden his slaves, nor cause them distress.' "[20]

Maimonides goes on to say:

Similarly, we should not embarrass a slave verbally or physically, for the Torah only contemplated work for them not humiliation. Nor should one excessively scream at or exhibit anger with them. Instead, one should speak to them gently, and listen to their complaints. This is explicitly stated with regard to the positive paths of Job

[19] Ibid., under "Maimonides and the Problem of Non-Israelite Slaves: *Mishneh Torah*". The definition of "harsh labor" (*pharekh*) is cited from *Mishneh Torah*, "Laws of Slaves", 1:6.

[20] Ibid. The quote from Maimonides is cited from *Mishneh Torah*, "Laws of Slaves", 9:8.

for which he was praised [in] Job 31:13, 15: "Have I ever shunned justice for my slave and maid-servant when they quarreled with me.... Did not He who made me in my mother's belly make him? Did not One form us both in the womb?"[21]

While Maimonides' previous *pharekh* observations endorsed supererogatory conduct, here he stresses abiding by the legal duties a master owes his slave because, as Job says, slaves and free Israelites share an important commonality: they share the same humanity since both are created from the same conjugal processes and are both formed in the womb.[22]

This is a significant change in the recognition and acknowledgment of the humanity of Gentile slaves. As Israel reflects on the Scriptures, there is a recognition of the deeper truth of what it means to be made in the image and likeness of God, which applies to all individuals and not just the Chosen People. There is a developmental shift that takes place where the blinders of "natural order" race subjugation are supplanted by the contemplation of race through a spiritual lens.

There is also a subtle recognition (that will become fully realized in Christ) that although Israel holds a special place in God's heart, all races are one in Him. The selective approach of engaging God's Word in order to justify racism is being replaced by a pronounced exegetical analysis that affirms race as a reflection of God's mercy and life-giving love.

---

[21] Quoted in ibid. The quote from Maimonides is cited from *Mishneh Torah*, "Laws of Slaves", 9:8.

[22] "If I have rejected the cause of my manservant or my maidservant, when they brought a complaint against me; what then shall I do when God rises up? ... Did not he who made me in the womb make him? And did not one fashion us in the womb?" Job 31:13–15.

Maimonides reflects this shifting race dynamic in his commentary on Psalm 145:9 ("The LORD is good to all, and his compassion is over all that he has made")[23] and Deuteronomy 13:18, where God will outpour His mercy "if you obey the voice of the LORD your God, keeping all his commandments which I command you this day, and doing what is right in the sight of the LORD your God."[24] According to Diamond, Maimonides uses mercy "to underline the moral of gravity of the benevolent treatment of slaves, regardless of their origins, by raising it to the level of *imitatio dei*".[25] Diamond notes that

> for Maimonides, material success or physical prowess do not in any way indicate superiority over others since they are simply arbitrary consequences of the natural world that do not constitute an "increment in substance." ... No verse better captures what is perceived as the modern liberal ideal of "all men are created equal" than Psalms 145:9 in Maimonides' reading. It elevates the equalization of another human being to a metaphysical standard of *imitatio dei*, and one which emulates the specific divine trait that grounds all of human existence in the "mercy" that establishes a common human form and that is blind to contingent differences.[26]

In the final analysis, Rabbi Moses Maimonides uses Scripture to show slavery's (and by association, racism's) absolute spiritual poverty. God's benevolent and superabundant

[23] For Maimonides' commentary on Psalm 145:9, see Diamond, "Treatment of Non-Israelite Slaves", under "Maimonides and Problem of Non-Israelite Slaves".

[24] For Maimonides' commentary on Deuteronomy 13:18, see ibid.

[25] Ibid., under "A Closer Look at the Verses Maimonides Quotes".

[26] Ibid., under "All Humans Are Created Equal: Maimonides in *Guide of the Perplexed*".

love, wisdom, and mercy are mirrored in the creatures made in His image and likeness from the moment of conception. God offers these gifts of Himself, rooted in covenant relationship, freely to all in which we make a gift of ourselves to others in love and sacrifice. However, as a result of the Fall, God's image has become blurred and distorted in us. To exercise the racist practice of enslavement—to exert dominance over human persons or subjugate other races—further distorts God's ascendency with the lie of the Evil One ("You will be like God"[27]) centered on a love turned in on itself. Thus, racism is an act *against* God rather than an imitation *of* God.

Final Thoughts

It should be noted that slavery was not mandated by God but, rather, it was regulated by the Israelites themselves. Slavery, for example, was used as punishment for criminal offenses, akin to community service done by inmates today. This practice is not wrong in itself and, in fact, could contribute to the individual's rehabilitation. In addition, the practice of slavery described above, where people would voluntarily engage in indentured servitude to pay off debt or feed themselves and their families, although appalling to modern sensibilities, was not intrinsically evil although, admittedly, this arrangement could have led to gravely sinful actions.

Catholic apologist Trent Horn further notes that "in ancient Rome freed slaves did not abandon their masters after settling into new employment. Instead, these slaves became 'clients' (*liberti*) and their former masters became

[27] Gen 3:5.

'patrons' (*patroni*) to whom they still owed loyalty, favors, and the fruit of their labor. Freed slaves usually took the name of their former master's family, and the client-patron relationship helped the *liberti* [slaves] overcome social stigmas and monetary hurdles that prevented them from climbing the Roman social ladder."[28]

Finally, in his letters, Saint Paul endeavors to address the deeply engrained institution of slavery across both social and cultural boundaries in first-century Rome. Roman civilization had some influence on the Christian view of slavery, and Paul understood that his apostolic responsibility included forming these early Christians with "the mind of Christ"[29], presenting a way of living that was contrary to societal norms. Paul's letters transmit a consistent, universal message of how early Christian communities should treat slaves.

Paul teaches in his First Letter to Timothy, "Let all who are under the yoke of slavery regard their masters as worthy of all honor, so that the name of God and the teaching may not be defamed. Those who have believing masters must not be disrespectful on the ground that they are brethren; rather they must serve all the better since those who benefit by their service are believers and beloved."[30] In Ephesians, Saint Paul teaches, "Slaves, be obedient to those who are your earthly masters, with fear and trembling, in singleness of heart, as to Christ; not in the way of eye-service, as men-pleasers, but as servants of Christ, doing the will of God from the heart, rendering service with a good will as to the Lord and not to men,

---

[28] Trent Horn, "Slavery and the New Testament", *Catholic Answers*, September 1, 2016, https://www.catholic.com/magazine/print-edition/slavery-and-the-new-testament.

[29] 1 Cor 2:16.

[30] 1 Tim 6:1–2.

knowing that whatever good any one does, he will receive the same again from the Lord, whether he is a slave or free."[31] In Colossians, he teaches, "Slaves, obey in everything those who are your earthly masters, not with eye-service, as men-pleasers, but in singleness of heart, fearing the Lord. Whatever your task, work heartily, as serving the Lord and not men, knowing that from the Lord you will receive the inheritance as your reward; you are serving the Lord Christ."[32]

That said, Saint Paul is unclear as to whether he is referring to chattel slavery or indentured servitude in his writings. He neither condemns the institution of slavery outright as an intrinsically moral evil, nor does he apply the teachings of Jesus specifically to the institution of slavery. Being well versed in the Jewish Scriptures, one would think that Paul would have at least condemned chattel slavery by appealing to the teachings of Jesus Christ as the new standard for society. The Lord teaches in the Gospel of Matthew, "Whatever you wish that men would do to you, do so to them; for this is the law and the prophets,"[33] and in the Gospel of Luke, "I say to you that hear, Love your enemies, do good to those who hate you, bless those who curse you, pray for those who abuse you."[34] Paul does, however, state in Galatians, "There is neither Jew nor Greek, there is neither slave nor free, there is neither male nor female; for you are all one in Christ Jesus,"[35] and in his Letter to Philemon, "Perhaps this is why he [Onesimus] was parted from you for a while, that you might have him back for ever, no longer as a slave but more than a

---

[31] Eph 6:5–8.
[32] Col 3:22–24.
[33] Mt 7:12.
[34] Lk 6:27.
[35] Gal 3:28.

slave, as a beloved brother, especially to me but how much more to you, both in the flesh and in the Lord."[36]

Although Saint Paul did not call for the abolition of slavery, he recognizes and acknowledges that we are all called to be one in the Body of Christ. New Testament scholar James Dunn summarizes how Saint Paul's strong preaching on unanimity among believers in Christ Jesus transcended cultural slavery and any racist ideology that accompanied it. Dunn states,

> The economies of the ancient world could not have functioned without slavery. Consequently, a responsible challenge to the practice of slavery would have required a complete reworking of the economic system and complete rethinking of social structures, which was scarcely thinkable at the time.... [Paul's] call for masters to treat their slaves "with justice and equity" assumes a higher degree of equality than was normal. And above all, the repeated reference to the primary relationship to the Lord (for both slave and free) highlights a fundamental criterion of human relationships which in the longer term was bound to undermine the institution itself.[37]

Slavery, as we define it today, did not have the same meaning or import as it did for ancient Israelites. Unlike chattel slavery practiced in the United States and other countries a century ago—and the modern-day slavery of human trafficking—slaves of the ancient Near East had rights, could become members of families, and, for the most part, were not treated with cruelty and humiliation. Old Testament slavery was not solely based on race, but

[36] Philem 3–4.
[37] James D. G. Dunn, *The Theology of Paul the Apostle* (Grand Rapids, Mich.: Eerdmans, 2006), 699, 701.

it must be acknowledged that Israelite slaves were treated differently than slaves of other races—this as a result of how Israel's covenant-status was understood, not as a consequence of race, per se. In the end, the teachings of our Lord Jesus Christ must serve as the foundation for overcoming racism of any kind—seeking justice and equality within the heart of God.

CHAPTER TWO

The Church's Historical Response to Racism

The Church's response to racism in the United States, both by the faithful and the Magisterium, was certainly uneven at best. Racism was both supported and condemned. In the nineteenth century, there were Catholic laity, religious orders, and bishops who owned and sold slaves. They actively promoted slavery to the point of distorting the Scriptures and papal statements to justify the practice. Sadly, this mentality persisted into the postbellum era through the support and enforcement of Jim Crow laws in the Church in twentieth-century America.

Conversely, there were continuous and consistent statements from the popes condemning the slave trade outright. Many Catholics were involved in the abolitionist movement and the Underground Railroad. Several American bishops and priests spoke out strongly against the brutal oppression and enslavement of people of color. They were willing to endure criticism and ridicule for their anti-slavery advocacy while simultaneously working toward emancipation for slaves and respect for the dignity of every human person.

Slavery has a complicated history and (as was mentioned in the previous chapter) the nations of the ancient world could not have functioned without it. The word "slavery", as we have seen, was used to describe the various manifestations of the practice, from forced labor to indentured servitude, spanning centuries of human history. The liberal use of the word "slavery" requires one, when examining the Church's response, to discern what type of slavery the Church is referring to. This is an important point since both the ancient and modern world economies depended on both types of slavery, and the Church's discordant response was shaped by both Catholic clergymen who were advocates of slavery and those who decried the practice.

Pro-Slavery Catholics

When the Church takes her eyes off the Cross of Christ and capitulates to cultural norms and ideologies for either economic benefit or to maintain the status quo, the People of God suffer. This occurred with slavery through the deliberate twisting of the Scriptures by pro-slavery Catholics.

The local Council of Gangra in A.D. 340 stated that "if anyone, on the pretext of godliness, teach a slave to scorn his master, and to leave his service, and not to afford his services to his own master with favor and all honor, let him be anathema."[1] Conciliar pronouncements like these, as well as Saint Paul's teachings on the treatment of slaves in his letters to the Ephesians and to Timothy (cited in previous chapter), have been used to justify the practice of chattel slavery. Father Cyprian Davis, O.S.B., in his landmark work *The History of Black Catholics in the United States*, notes that in the United States "some of

---

[1] The Council of Gangra, Canon 3, from "The Canons of the Eastern Orthodox Church", Google, accessed December 13, 2022, https://sites.google.com/site/canonsoc/home/-canons-of-the-particular-councils/gangra-council-340.

the Southern bishops ... considered themselves as apologists for slavery, obligated to defend it on the basis of Catholic tradition and Scripture."[2]

Father Davis also notes that "slavery was very much an accepted institution in the world of the sixteenth and seventeenth centuries. It was accepted as an institution by the church leaders of the time, despite the efforts of popes to regulate trafficking in slaves and of Catholic theologians to determine the legitimate basis for the enslavement of certain peoples."[3] In many European countries, the legislation of slavery by the Church was rooted in Christian Roman law. Slave owners, for example, were obliged to baptize their slaves and ensure they practiced the faith, not only in the Sunday obligation but in all aspects, including marriage and family life. Christian Roman law also determined who could be enslaved. These individuals typically included war captives, convicted criminals, and those with extraordinary family circumstances. Rev. Joel S. Panzer notes that

> the rules of war and society were such that servitude was often imposed as a penalty on criminals and prisoners of war, and was even freely chosen by many workers for economic reasons. Children born of those held in servitude were also at times considered to be in the same state as that of their parents. These types of servitude were the most common among those generally considered to establish the so called "just titles" of servitude. In such cases, it must be noted that the Church was always adamant about the obligation of masters to give fair and humane treatment to those held in servitude, and even encouraged their liberation.[4]

[2] Cyprian Davis, O.S.B., *The History of Black Catholics in the United States* (New York: Crossroad Publishing, 1990), 46.

[3] Ibid., 20.

[4] Joel S. Panzer, *The Popes and Slavery* (New York: Alba House, 1996), 3.

Despite the incorporation of the rule of law, Father Davis notes that the "fact that one individual had ownership of the person and the labor of another provided the framework for inevitable acts of oppression and brutality".[5] The secular culture, inspired by greed and avarice, forced individuals into slavery against their will. There was a deliberate and total disregard for human rights and dignity, and according to Dr. Jaime Luciano Balmes, "Slaves were compelled to obey, not on account of superior motives or moral obligations, but because they were the property of their masters, horses governed by the bridle, and mere mechanical machines."[6]

Slave owners had the power of life and death over their slaves, and often abused this power out of caprice, hatred, or whim. Violence and brutalization became the hallmark of chattel slavery. Dr. Balmes notes that the tyrannical oppression of slavery could be traced back to antiquity and quotes the Roman senator Cassius regarding the treatment of foreign slaves, who "can only be restrained by terror".[7] This was particularly true of slavery in America.

One may have thought the Church in the United States would have been vehemently against chattel slavery and worked tirelessly for its eradication. While this was true in some parts of the country, there were many Catholic laypersons, clergy, and religious orders who defended slavery, justifying it by integrating the historic Christian Roman law into the slave practice. According to Father Davis, "In 1836 the general of the Jesuits, John Roothaan, approved

[5] Davis, *History of Black Catholics in United States*, 20.

[6] Jaime Luciano Balmes, *European Civilization: Protestantism and Catholicity Compared*, trans. C.J. Hanford and Robert Kershaw (Baltimore: Murphy, 1850), 74. Original Spanish edition: Jaime Luciano Balmes, *El Protestantismo Comparado Con El Catolicismo* (Barcelona: Brusi, 1849).

[7] Ibid., 75.

the sale of slaves, provided the practice of the Catholic faith by the slaves was assured and that families were not separated."[8] This arrangement was by no means guaranteed and, in many cases, not honored as slaves were often sold to non-Catholic slave owners.

As previously stated, religious orders operating in America owned slaves. Father Davis notes that

> the Vincentian superior, Felix DeAndreis, justified the ownership of slaves because there were no lay brothers to perform the manual labor and because other seminaries ... had female slaves for domestic work.... The Vincentians had the policy of selling, hiring, and lending their slaves among the various houses and parishes....
>
> The Sulpicians had slaves in their seminaries in Baltimore and Bardstown, Kentucky. The Capuchins in Louisiana owned slaves as well....
>
> The Ursuline nuns who came to New Orleans in 1727 owned slaves from the beginning.... The Carmelite nuns ... owned slaves, [as] part of the dowry of incoming novices.[9]

A major pro-slavery victory was achieved when in 1857 the Supreme Court ruled in *Dred Scott v. John F. Sanford* that black people could be property and were not citizens of the United States. The attitude generated by this decision, although abrogated by the Emancipation Proclamation and Thirteenth Amendment to the Constitution, would have major repercussions throughout the twentieth century and beyond.

Chief Justice Roger B. Taney, the first Catholic to serve on the Supreme Court, was born into a wealthy,

---

[8] Davis, *History of Black Catholics in United States*, 37.
[9] Ibid., 38–39.

slave-owning family. In his majority opinion, Chief Justice Taney outlined a political, moral, and philosophical stance that would have far-reaching legal, economic, sociological, and psychological implications and effects for decades to come. I quote him at length so the reader can absorb the full impact of his argumentation:

> A free negro of the African race, whose ancestors were brought to this country and sold as slaves, is not a "citizen" within the meaning of the Constitution of the United States....
>
> In the opinion of the court, the legislation and histories of the times, and the language used in the Declaration of Independence, show, that neither the class of persons who had been imported as slaves, nor their descendants, whether they had become free or not, were then acknowledged as a part of the people, nor intended to be included in the general words used in that memorable instrument....
>
> They had for more than a century before been regarded as beings of an inferior order, and altogether unfit to associate with the white race, either in social or political relations; and so far inferior, that they had no rights which the white man was bound to respect; and that the negro might justly and lawfully be reduced to slavery for his benefit. He was bought and sold, and treated as an ordinary article of merchandise and traffic, whenever a profit could be made by it. This opinion was at that time fixed and universal in the civilized portion of the white race. It was regarded as an axiom in morals as well as in politics, which no one thought of disputing, or supposed to be open to dispute; and men in every grade and position in society daily and habitually acted upon it in their private pursuits, as well as in matters of public concern; without doubting for a moment the correctness of this opinion....
>
> They show that a perpetual and impassable barrier was intended to be erected between the white race and the one which they had reduced to slavery, and governed as

subjects with absolute and despotic power, and which they then looked upon as so far below them in the scale of created beings, that intermarriages between white persons and negroes or mulattoes were regarded as unnatural and immoral, and punished as crimes, not only in the parties, but in the person who joined them in marriage. And no distinction in this respect was made between the free negro or mulatto and the slave, but this stigma, of the deepest degradation, was fixed upon the whole race....

But it is too clear for dispute, that the enslaved African race were not intended to be included, and formed no part of the people who framed and adopted this declaration; for if the language, as understood in that day, would embrace them, the conduct of the distinguished men who framed the Declaration of Independence would have been utterly and flagrantly inconsistent with the principles they asserted; and instead of the sympathy of mankind, to which they so confidently appealed, they would have deserved and received universal rebuke and reprobation....

The unhappy black race were separated from the white by indelible marks, and laws long before established, and were never thought of or spoken of except as property, and when the claims of the owner or the profit of the trader were supposed to need protection.[10]

Where was the response of the Church to the overt racism of this decision? Where was the condemnation of Chief Justice Taney? Where was the moral outcry of the Catholic faithful?

One of the factors of the pathetic response of the Church in America was that a good number of bishops owned slaves and actively engaged in the slave trade

[10] State Historical Society of Iowa, "U.S. Supreme Court Majority Opinion on Dred Scott v. John Sanford Case, March 6, 1857", I.4, V.2, IowaCulture.Gov, accessed December 13, 2021, https://iowaculture.gov/sites/default/files/history-education-pss-equality-dred-transcription.pdf.

along with many priests and religious. According to Father Davis, "Louis William DuBourg as a bishop in the Louisiana Territory had no problems ... profiting from the slavery system.... He was willing to use his slaves as collateral to borrow money and as investments for other financial ventures."[11] One of the most notorious pro-slavery prelates was Bishop John England of Charleston, South Carolina. He "sought to show with arguments from history, Scripture, the canons of church councils and local synods, and finally canon law and Roman law that slavery had always existed and been accepted as legitimate under specific titles or circumstances."[12] He concluded that since the Church permitted slavery "it is impossible to believe that the scriptures or the church would have treated slavery without condemning it, if it was fundamentally wrong."[13]

Father Davis points out the speciousness of this position:

The legislation in the Old Testament, the canons of the church councils, the jurisprudence of Roman law, and the teaching of the popes all sought to ameliorate the condition of slaves and to recognize the existence of certain rights that accrued to the person of the slave, especially regarding marriage, family life, freedom from sexual exploitation, and even certain property rights. The slavery system in the Southern states recognized no such rights inherent in the slave as a person, no freedom regarding marriage, no freedom regarding religious practice, and turned a blind eye to arbitrary penalties and sanctions by slaveholders, who were in no way bound to respect the personality and humanity of the slave.[14]

---

[11] Davis, *History of Black Catholics in United States*, 43.

[12] Ibid., 47. "Canon law" here refers to the body of Church law and governance prior to the promulgation of the 1917 Code of Canon Law.

[13] Ibid.

[14] Ibid.

Bishop Auguste Marie Martin of Natchitoches, Louisiana, described slavery as a blessing in disguise for people of color. He stated that chattel slavery was not evil but "a betterment both material and moral for a degraded class".[15] Bishop Augustin Verot of Saint Augustine, Florida, argued that Sacred Scripture clearly showed "that the prophets, apostles, and even the Lord himself spoke of slaves and about slaves and slavery, and in fact ameliorated the condition of slavery but significantly never condemned its existence, although the opportunity was there to do so. The same argument was used from church history. The church called for regulation and never enjoined condemnation, which would have been done were slavery inherently evil."[16] Hence, many American Catholics, including those in leadership roles, conflated the fluid term "slavery" and manipulated the meaning of Church statements in order to advance their agenda. This is not the Catholic faith.

Antislavery Catholics

The Catholic Church, through her Magisterium, has spoken out against chattel slavery throughout her entire history. Other forms of "slavery" mentioned above were not evil under all circumstances, or evil per se, and, as such, were not condemned outright. In these cases, the Church, through local synods and papal teaching, sought to ensure that the dignity of slaves was respected and protected. Dr. Balmes observed that the Church "devoted all her efforts to improve as much as possible the condition of slaves; in punishments she caused mildness to be substituted for

[15] Quoted in ibid., 51–52.
[16] Quoted in ibid., 53.

cruelty; next and what was more important than all, she laboured to put reason in the place of caprice, and to make the impetuosity of masters yield to the coolness of judges; that is to say, she every day assimilated the condition of slaves more and more to that of freemen, by making right and not might reign over them."[17]

The Church's effort in this regard was extensive. Here are a few examples from local European synods spanning seven centuries:[18]

Council of Elvira (Spain, beginning of the fourth century A.D.) punished those who caused a slave's death.

Council of Orange (A.D. 441) censured anyone who tried to reenslave emancipated individuals within the church enclosure.

Council of Ireland (A.D. 451) ordered that clerics must use their own money to emancipate slaves rather than steal them.

Council of Epaone (A.D. 517) imposed a two-year excommunication for masters who put their slaves to death.

Council of Orleans (A.D. 549) excommunicated a slave owner for punishing a slave who took refuge in a church.

Council of Lyons (A.D. 566) excommunicated anyone who unjustly enslaved a free person.

Council of Lyon (A.D. 583) authorized the Church to issue freedom papers for slaves.

Council of Macon (A.D. 585) authorized the use of Church property to free slaves.

Council of Toledo (A.D. 589) ordered that slaves shall not be denied protection from the Church.

---

[17] Balmes, *European Civilization*, 75.
[18] See ibid., 76–87.

Council of Rome (A.D. 595) ordered that freed slaves could enter monastic life.

Council of Boneuil (France, A.D. 616) encouraged Catholics to gift or lend money toward the freedom of slaves.

Council of Rheims (A.D. 625) banned the creation of new slaves and authorized the use of Church property to free current slaves.

Fourth Council of Toledo (A.D. 633) ordered that freed slaves can be ordained clerics.

Council of Merida (A.D. 666) banned the mutilation of slaves.

Council of Celchite (England, A.D. 816) ordered that at a bishop's death, all his slaves must be freed.

Council of Verneuil (A.D. 844) authorized the use of Church property to free slaves.

Council of Worms (A.D. 868) imposed a two-year penance for masters who put their slaves to death.

Council of Coblentz (A.D. 922) defined the slave trade as homicide.

Council of Armagh (A.D. 1172) granted liberty to all English slaves held in Ireland.

When juxtaposed with the constant, unwavering position of the papal Magisterium of the Church that has condemned chattel slavery outright, there can be no doubt of the Church's vigorous stance against the deliberate deprivation of human liberty and the cruel inhumanity of the slave trade.

Antislavery Catholics: Papal Statements

Pope after pope, including Clement I, Pius II, Eugene IV, Gregory XIV, Innocent XI, Benedict XIV, Pius VII, and many others, have strongly advocated against slavery, describing it as immoral, inhuman, and the enemy of the human race.

These papal declarations were promulgated in Latin. The Latin word *servitus* can be translated as both "servitude" and "slavery". In this regard, Father Panzer writes,

> When speaking of the *servitus* which rested on one of the so-called "just titles" [i.e., criminals, prisoners of war or freely chosen, as described above], we translate the Latin as "servitude"; when speaking of that form of *servitus* which did not rest on just title [i.e., forced labor against one's will], we translate the Latin as "slavery." In the Magisterial documents ... the institution of slavery is referred to by such Latin phrases as *servituti subicere* (to *subject* to slavery), or, more commonly, *in servitutem redigere* (to *reduce* to slavery). By the use of such terms, the documents are referring to *servitus* in its unjust and most commonly understood form.[19]

The following are several examples of papal statements denouncing slavery.

In 1434, the Vatican became aware of enslavement occurring in the newly colonized Canary Islands. In January 1435, Pope Eugene IV issued *Sicut Dudum*, where he specifically identifies the immoral behavior occurring on the islands and forthrightly condemns the activity:

> They [the Christian colonizers] have deprived the natives of their property or turned it to their own use, and have subjected some of the inhabitants of said islands to perpetual slavery (*subdiderunt perpetuae servituti*), sold them to other persons and committed other various illicit and evil

---

[19] Panzer, *Popes and Slavery*, 5–6.

deeds against them.... Therefore We ... to rebuke each
sinner about his sin ... with a holy and fatherly concern,
for the sufferings of the inhabitants, beseech in the Lord
and exhort ... that they themselves desist from the afore-
mentioned deeds.... We order and command all and each
of the faithful of each sex that, within the span of fifteen
days of the publication of these letters ... they restore to
their earlier liberty all and each person of either sex who
were once residents of said Canary Islands and make captives since the time of their capture and who have been
made subject to slavery (*servituti subditos habent*). These
people are to be totally and perpetually free and are to be
let go without the exaction or reception of any money. If
this is not done ... they will incur the sentence of excommunication *ipso facto*, from which they cannot be absolved,
except at the point of death, even by the Holy See.... We
will that like sentence of excommunication be incurred
by one and all who attempt to capture or sell or subject to
slavery (*servituti subicere*) baptized residents of the Canary
Islands or those who are freely seeking baptism.[20]

In his 1537 encyclical *Sublimis Deus*, 320 years before
Dred Scott, Pope Paul III excommunicated those who
enslaved the Indians of the Americas. He states,

> We ... by our Apostolic Authority decree and declare by
> these present letters that the same Indians and all other
> peoples—even though they are outside the faith—who
> shall hereafter come to the knowledge of Christians have
> not been deprived or should not be deprived of their lib-
> erty or of their possessions. Rather they are to be able to
> use and enjoy this liberty and this ownership of property
> freely and licitly, and are not to be reduced to slavery (*nec*

[20] Ibid., 76–78, citing Eugene IV, *Sicut Dudum* (January 13, 1435), in Baro-
nius, *Annales Ecclesiastici*, ed. O. Raynaldus (Luca, 1752), 28:226–27.

in servitutem redigi debere), and that whatever happens to the contrary is to be considered null and void and as having no force of law.[21]

Also, in 1537 in his apostolic brief *Pastorale Officium*, he declares that

> anyone of whatever dignity, state, condition or grade who works against what is done through you or others to help the Indians in the aforementioned matters incurs the penalty of excommunication *latae sententiae*, incurred ipso facto.... This is done so that no one in any way may presume to reduce said Indians to slavery (*in servitutem redigere*) or despoil them of their goods.[22]

The final example from Pope Gregory XVI should have removed all of the excuses from the pro-slavery Catholics in America. *In Supremo* is an encyclical letter issued to the universal Church specifically condemning the African slave trade. After detailing the antislavery teachings of his predecessors, the Holy Father says,

> We still say it with sorrow, there were to be found subsequently among the faithful some who, shamefully blinded by the desire of sordid gain ... did not hesitate to reduce to the slavery Indians, Blacks and other unfortunate peoples, or else, by instituting or expanding the trade in those who have been made slaves by others, aided the crime of others.... Our Predecessors did not fail, according to the duties of their office, to blame severely this way of acting

[21] Pope Paul III, *Sublimis Deus* (June 2, 1537), quoted in Panzer, *Popes and Slavery*, 80–81, citing *Las Casas En Mexico: Historia y obras desconocidas*, by Helen-Rand Parish and Harold E. Weidman (Mexico City: Fondo De Cultura Economica, 1992), 310–11.

[22] Pope Paul III, apostolic brief *Pastorale Officium* to Juan Cardinal de Tavera of Toledo (May 29, 1537), quoted in Panzer, *Popes and Slavery*, 85, citing *Coleccion de Bulas*, by Francisco Javier Hernáez (Bruselas: A. Vromant, 1879), 101–2.

as dangerous for the spiritual welfare of those who did such things and a shame to the Christian name.... Therefore, desiring to remove such a great shame from all Christian peoples,... and walking in the footsteps of Our Predecessors, We, by apostolic authority, warn and strongly exhort in the Lord faithful Christians of every condition that no one in the future dare to bother unjustly, despoil of their possessions, or reduce to slavery (*in servitutem redigere*) Indians, Blacks or other such peoples. Nor are they to lend aid and favor to those who give themselves up to these practices or exercise that inhuman traffic by which the Blacks, as if they were not humans but rather mere animals,... are, without any distinction and contrary to the rights of justice and humanity, bought, sold and sometimes given over to the hardest labor.... We then, by Apostolic Authority, condemn all such practices as absolutely unworthy of the Christian name. By the same Authority We prohibit and strictly forbid any Ecclesiastic or layperson from presuming to defend as permissible this trade in Blacks under no matter what pretext or excuse, or from publishing or teaching in any manner whatsoever, in public or privately, opinions contrary to what we have set forth.[23]

In Supremo stands in stark contradiction to the *Dred Scott* decision, issued eighteen years later, and clearly shows the arrogant indifference of some American Catholics who ignored the magisterial teaching of the popes. Pro-slavery Catholics cannot possibly claim that Gregory XVI's encyclical did not pertain to the United States or to Christian slave owners. They instead freely chose to remain blind and ignorant, serving the culture and their own self-interest instead of Christ.

There is one papal document in particular, Pope Nicholas V's 1452 bull *Dum Diversas*, that is highly controversial

[23] Pope Gregory XVI, *In Supremo* (December 3, 1839), quoted in Panzer, *Popes and Slavery*, 98–99, 101–2, citing Hernáez, *Coleccion de Bulas*, 114–16.

and seems to contradict other papal writings regarding slavery. The document is mentioned briefly in the United States Conference of Catholic Bishops' 2018 pastoral letter *Open Wide Our Hearts: The Enduring Call to Love*, where it is described as "setting the stage for the slave trade".[24] This statement is made without any citation or context and deserves a brief analysis.

The "slave trade" commonly refers to the transatlantic slave trade between Africa, the Americas, and the Caribbean. Slavery, however, existed on the continent of Africa long before European involvement, and it is one of a number of factors that contributed to slavery becoming transcontinental. In "Slavery before the Trans-Atlantic Trade" by the Lowcountry Digital History Initiative (a digital public history project), the article comments that

> slavery was prevalent in many West and Central African societies before and during the trans-Atlantic slave trade. When diverse African empires, small to medium-sized nations, or kinship groups came into conflict for various political and economic reasons, individuals from one African group regularly enslaved captives from another group because they viewed them as outsiders. The rulers of these slaveholding societies could then exert power over these captives as prisoners of war for labor needs, to expand their kinship group or nation, influence and disseminate spiritual beliefs, or potentially to trade for economic gain.[25]

[24] United States Conference of Catholic Bishops, Committee on Cultural Diversity, *Open Wide Our Hearts: The Enduring Call to Love; A Pastoral Letter against Racism* (Washington, D.C.: United States Conference of Catholic Bishops, 2018), 21, https://www.usccb.org/issues-and-action/human-life-and-dignity/racism/upload/open-wide-our-hearts.pdf.

[25] Lowcountry Digital History Initiative, "Slavery before the Trans-Atlantic Trade", under "Slavery in West and Central Africa", Lowcountry Digital Library, College of Charleston, accessed December 13, 2021, http://ldhi.library.cofc.edu/exhibits/show/africanpassageslowcountryadapt/introduction atlanticworld/slaverybeforetrade.

A major part of African history is the Eastern and trans-Saharan slave trade. David Gakunzi states that "the deportation of Africans to the lands of Islam was structured around two main roads: the maritime traffic between the coast of East Africa and those of the Middle East on the one hand, and the trans-Saharan caravan traffic on the other."[26] He goes on to note that this slave trade

> lasted more than 13 centuries. It began in the early seventh century and continued in one form or another until the 1960s....
>
> The Arab slave trade was characterized by appalling violence, castration, and rape. The men were systematically castrated to prevent them from reproducing and becoming a stock. This inhumane practice resulted in a high death rate: six out of 10 people who were mutilated died from their wounds in castration centers. The Arab slave trade also targeted African women and girls, who were captured and deported for use as sex slaves.
>
> According to the work of some historians, the Arab slave trade has affected more than 17 million people. In the Saharan region alone, more than nine million African captives were deported and two million died on the roads.[27]

Another important factor was the introduction of Portuguese traders to the African continent. According to the Lowcountry Digital History Initiative, the Portuguese mariner "Antam Gonçalvez, who sailed to West Africa in 1441 hoping to acquire seal skins and oil ... led a raiding party into Cap Blanc, a narrow peninsula between Western Sahara and Mauritania, and kidnapped two Berbers,

---

[26] David Gakunzi, "The Arab-Muslim Slave Trade: Lifting the Taboo", *Jewish Political Studies Review* 29, nos. 3–4 (September 3, 2018), https://jcpa.org /article/the-arab-muslim-slave-trade-lifting-the-taboo/.

[27] Ibid.

one man and one woman. Another Portuguese mariner, Nuno Tristão, and members of his crew soon joined Gonçalvez",[28] resulting in the acquisition of approximately twelve captives. This incident is widely considered to be the start of the African slave trade.

This historical background is important to understanding the reason the papal bull *Dum Diversas* was issued. It is not a document about slavery. Pope Nicholas V issued *Dum Diversas* in 1452 in response to the very specific concerns of Alfonse, king of Portugal.

Alfonse had written to the Holy Father asking for permission to move forward with a rather aggressive plan to address "the enemies of Christ"—the Saracens or Arab Muslims—and convert them to Catholicism.[29] In response, the pope granted full authority for Alfonse "to invade, conquer, fight, subjugate the Saracens and Pagans, and other infidels and other enemies of Christ ... and to lead their persons in perpetual servitude (*illorumque personas in perpetuam servitutem redigendi*)".[30]

The use of the Latin phrase *servitutem redigendi* indicates that the pope authorized the enslavement of the Saracens against their will. Why would he do this? There are four factors to consider:

---

[28] Lowcountry Digital History Initiative, "Pope Nicolas V and the Portuguese Slave Trade", accessed December 15, 2022, http://ldhi.library.cofc.edu /exhibits/show/african_laborers_for_a_new_emp/pope_nicolas_v_and _the_portugu.

[29] "Christi nominis inimicorum rabies Christi fidelibus in orthodoxae vilipendium fidei semper infesta reprimi, Christianaeque Religioni valeat subjugari ... fidem ipsam defendere ... tu Christi inimicos Sarracenos videlicet, subjugare, ac ad Christi fidem potenti ..." Nicolaus V, "Dum Diversas" (18 de junho de 1452), quoted in *Bullarium Patronatus Portugalliae Regum, Tomus I, 1171–1600*, ed. Levy Maria Jordão (Lisbon: Olisipone), MDCCCLXVIII, 22.

[30] "... sanctissimo proposito confovere merito cupientes, tibi Sarracenos, et Paganos, aliosque infidels, et Christi inimicos quoscunque ... illorumque personas in perpetuam servitutem redigendi." Quoted in ibid.

1. *Dum Diversas* authorized *only* the king of Portugal to carry out a preemptive strike to counter the hostility of the Saracens and other "enemies of Christ", and not to exercise the use of force against innocent African peoples or tribes indiscriminately as Gonçalvez and Tristão had done. There was a long record of mistrust and enmity between Christians and Muslims going back to the time of the Crusades, and the belief in a "just war" may have been a factor in the pope's decision.

2. There is no specific wording in the document about buying, selling, or trading slaves, although, it must be admitted, the papal bull implicitly gave Alfonse authority to do so. However, the historical record is quite unclear as to whether Alfonse actually enslaved anyone.[31]

3. *Dum Diversas* authorized forced servitude, but there is nothing in the document that indicates the "enemies of Christ" are to be subjected to chattel slavery rather than indentured servitude.

4. Since what was set forth in *Dum Diversas* was not universally taught, it does not rise to the level of authority described as universal magisterial teaching. As a result, the tenets of this papal bull are not necessary for belief by the faithful.

There is no getting around it: *Dum Diversas* is without doubt questionable but is, in reality, a fly on the windshield of the faith, so to speak. Popes can, and do, make poor prudential judgments, as do all of us at times. We are sinners in

---

[31] Biographies of Alfonse V's life and military record/exploits mention *Dum Diversas* but do not explicitly state that Alfonse subjugated prisoners of war to slavery. See, for example, https://www.britannica.com/biography /Nicholas-V-pope.

need of God's mercy. The bottom line is that *Dum Diversas* (and the later document *Romanus Pontifex* issued in 1455 by Pope Nicholas V) should not be given the same attention and focus as the overwhelming majority of authoritative papal teachings that denounce slavery outright.

Courageous Catholics

There were many faithful clergy and laity who jeopardized their reputations, livelihoods, and sacred offices in service of the truth.

In 1544 in an attempt to implement the antislavery teaching of Pope Paul III in *Sublimis Deus* (issued in 1537), Bishop Bartolomé de Las Casas of Chiapas, Mexico, "issued instructions to the priests who heard the confessions of slaveholders. Those who own slaves could not receive absolution from their sins until they promise to grant them freedom and ... made restitution to slaves from whom the slaveholders had unjustly profited",[32] as noted by Father Davis. The bishop was met with violent opposition and protests from both clerics and the faithful, resulting in Bishop Las Casas resigning from his See.

Saint Paul teaches that "where sin increased, grace abounded all the more."[33] During the dark days of slavery in North America, God raised up saints who served the poorest of the poor. The Jesuit priest Alonso Sandoval "spoke out forcefully against the conditions of black slaves in the Spanish colonies" and "was among the Jesuits who ministered to the slaves and also wrote a treatise excoriating the treatment they received at the

[32] Davis, *History of Black Catholics in United States*, 21–22.
[33] Rom 5:20.

hands of the slaveholders",[34] according to Father Davis. Sandoval's colleague Father Peter Claver worked diligently to improve the corporal and spiritual welfare of slaves in the United States, while his contemporary Dominican brother Martin de Porres did the same for the poor and oppressed in South America.

In 1862, Father Claude Paschal Maistre, a priest of New Orleans, began to oppose the slave trade adamantly. When his congregation complained to the archbishop, Father Maistre was suspended. He subsequently "ignored the suspension", and when Father Maistre "noted that in the parish registers there would no longer be a separation between the entries of whites and blacks",[35] he was placed under interdict. He was later reconciled to the Church after the Vatican intervened. At this same time, Archbishop John Baptist Purcell of Cincinnati, Ohio, spoke out boldly for the emancipation of slaves both in his public comments and in the archdiocesan newspaper, the *Catholic Telegraph*.

More could be said about the many nameless Catholic men and women who sacrificed their lives as abolitionists or conductors along the Underground Railroad to help slaves. There are also numerous religious sisters and priests who lived and worked among the slaves, providing an elementary education in both academia and the faith. Their heroic efforts should be acknowledged and remembered. Despite their hard work and best intentions, as Father Davis observes, "the Catholic church [*sic*] in the United States found itself incapable of taking any decisive action or enunciating clearly thought-out principles regarding slavery."[36] It would be several more decades before the

[34] Davis, *History of Black Catholics in United States*, 24.
[35] Ibid., 65.
[36] Ibid., 66.

hierarchy of the Church responded to racism as one collective voice.

The United States Bishops Respond to Racism

After World War II, individual bishops took stands against segregation, especially in Catholic schools, and religious orders began accepting black candidates. Then, in the period immediately preceding the civil rights movement, the United States bishops issued the pastoral letter *Discrimination and Christian Conscience* (1958), in which they state:

> The heart of the race question is moral and religious.... If our attitude is governed by the great Christian law of love of neighbor and respect for his rights, then we can work out harmoniously the techniques for making legal, educational, economic and social adjustments. But if our hearts are poisoned by hatred, or even indifference toward the welfare and rights of our fellow men, then our nation faces a grave internal crisis....
>
> We hope and earnestly pray that responsible and sober-minded Americans of all religious faiths, in all areas of our land, will seize the mantel of leadership from the agitator and the racist. It is vital that we act now and act decisively. All must act quietly, courageously and prayerfully before it is too late.[37]

These were bold statements given the entrenched Jim Crow laws at the time. This was the first courageous

[37] United States Catholic Bishops, *Discrimination and Christian Conscience* (November 14, 1958), from "Selected Quotes from *Discrimination and Christian Conscience*", USCCB.org, https://www.usccb.org/committees/ad-hoc -committee-against-racism/selected-quotes-discimination-and-christian-con science. Quotes were originally compiled by the Catholic News Service, August 25, 2017.

step taken by the bishops as a unified body to overcome the segregation that had made its way into the Catholic churches. The pastoral letter turns the heart of the racial question toward the natural moral law and everyone's equal place in the family of God. The bishops were not concerned with how they would be perceived by society or about capitulating to political correctness. The document, tinged with a sense of urgency, focused the faithful's attention back on what it means to be a true disciple of Christ. *Discrimination and Christian Conscience* was a small but significant step forward.

There have been other United States Catholic bishops' statements on race from the sixties to the present day. One of the most significant was the 1979 pastoral letter on racism, *Brothers and Sisters to Us*, where the bishops said:

> Racism is an evil which endures in our society and in our Church. Despite apparent advances and even significant changes in the last two decades, the reality of racism remains. In large part it is only external appearances which have changed. In 1958 we spoke out against the blatant forms of racism that divided people through discriminatory laws and enforced segregation. We pointed out the moral evil that denied human persons their dignity as children of God and their God-given rights. (1) A decade later in a second pastoral letter we again underscored the continuing scandal of racism [and] called for decisive action to eradicate it from our society. (2) We recognize and applaud the readiness of many Americans to make new strides forward in reducing and eliminating prejudice against minorities. We are convinced that the majority of Americans realize that racial discrimination is both unjust and unworthy of this nation. . . .
>
> Racism is a sin: a sin that divides the human family, blots out the image of God among specific members of that family, and violates the fundamental human dignity

of those called to be children of the same Father. Racism is the sin that says some human beings are inherently superior and others essentially inferior because of races. It is the sin that makes racial characteristics the determining factor for the exercise of human rights. It mocks the words of Jesus: "Treat the others the way you would have them treat you." (4) Indeed, racism is more than a disregard for the words of Jesus; it is a denial of the truth of the dignity of each human being revealed by the mystery of the Incarnation.[38]

Here, the bishops acknowledge their efforts to address racism over several decades, and their statements show increasing clarity, confidence, and resolve. By calling racism "evil" and "sin", the United States bishops teach clearly that it has no place whatsoever in the life of the Church and is antithetical to the message of Christ. *Brothers and Sisters to Us* makes a shift in emphasis from racism as a societal sin to a personal one. The bishops call us to see the image and likeness of God in one another and to follow the Golden Rule established by Jesus. *Brothers and Sisters to Us* called Catholics to be more mindful and aware of racial inequity and division, but the zeal and desire from the heart of the faithful to make this a reality remained a work in progress.

On September 9, 1984, the feast of Saint Peter Claver, the ten black bishops of the United States at that time issued a ground-breaking document on evangelization and the black Catholic community called *What We Have Seen and Heard*. In that letter, the bishops write:

[38] National Conference of Catholic Bishops, *Brothers and Sisters to Us: U.S. Catholic Bishops' Pastoral Letter on Racism* (Washington, D.C.: United States Catholic Conference, 1979), https://www.usccb.org/committees/african-american -affairs/brothers-and-sisters-us.

Black people know what freedom is because we remember the dehumanizing force of slavery, racist prejudice and oppression. No one can understand so well the meaning of the proclamation that Christ has set us free than those who have experienced the denial of freedom. For us, therefore, freedom is a cherished gift. For its preservation, no sacrifice is too great.

Hence, freedom brings responsibility. It must never be abused, equated with license nor taken for granted. Freedom is God's gift, and we are accountable to him for our loss of it. And we are accountable for the gift of freedom in the lives of others. We oppose all oppression and all injustice, for unless *all* are free *none* are free.[39]

What We Have Seen and Heard was released during my freshman year in college, and I remember the excitement it generated among black Catholics. It was a call to close the fissure of racial division and provided an evangelization roadmap that gave direction to parishes on how best to serve Catholics of color. It discussed areas of evangelization that were—and still are—critically important to black communities including abortion, vocations, education, and liturgy. The pastoral letter also considered two topics of particular significance, providing greater depth and insight to the discourse on race: black spirituality and the family.

What We Have Seen and Heard introduced the Church in the United States to black spirituality, comprised of four constitutive characteristics: it is contemplative, holistic, joyful, and communitarian.

[39] Joseph L. Howze et al., *"What We Have Seen and Heard": A Pastoral Letter on Evangelization from the Black Bishops of the United States* (Cincinnati: St. Anthony Messenger Press, 1984), 6 (emphasis in original), http://www.usccb.org/issues-and-action/cultural-diversity/african-american/resources/upload/what-we-have-seen-and-heard.pdf.

Black Spirituality is contemplative. By this we mean that prayer is spontaneous and pervasive in the Black tradition.... Black Spirituality senses the awe of God's transcendence and the vital intimacy of his closeness....

In an age of competition and control, we have learned to surrender to God's love and to let him work his power through us....

Black spirituality ... is holistic.... Divisions between intellect and emotion, spirit and body, action and contemplation, individual and community, sacred and secular are foreign to us.... For us, the religious experiences is an experience of the whole human being—both the feelings and the intellect, the heart as well as the head....

Joy is the hallmark of Black Spirituality. Joy is first of all celebration. Celebration is movement and song, rhythm and feeling, color and sensation, exultation and thanksgiving. We celebrate the presence and the proclamation of the Word....

The sense of community is a major component of Black Spirituality....

The communal dimension of our spirituality is a gift we also need to share.... The communal dimension of Black Spirituality permeates our experience of liturgy and worship....

Community, however, means social concern and social justice. Black Spirituality never excludes concern for human suffering and other people's concerns.[40]

The last decade of the twentieth century yielded *Love Thy Neighbor As Thyself: U.S. Catholic Bishops Speak against Racism*[41] in response to the call for the bishops to

[40] Ibid., 8–10.

[41] National Conference of Catholic Bishops, Committee on African American Catholics, *Love Thy Neighbor As Thyself: U.S. Catholic Bishops Speak against Racism; January 1997–June 2000* (Washington, D.C.: United States Catholic Conference, 2001).

increase their efforts to combat racism. The document contains a series of essays on various aspects of the issue, including the experience of Asian, Native American, and Hispanic/Latino communities. The question of race is examined through the lens of Catholic social teaching, liturgical expressions, immigration, hate crimes,[42] and ecumenism. *Love Thy Neighbor As Thyself* ends with a call to action for healing the sin of racism, including a nine-step outline by the Most Reverend Harry J. Flynn, archbishop emeritus of Saint Paul-Minneapolis. These elements include "(1) Realize it is a sin. (2) Be open to a change of heart. (3) Don't give in to xenophobia. (4) Avoid racial stereotypes, slurs, jokes. Bring the same to the attention of families and among friends. (5) Speak out against racial negatives. (6) In parishes, make sure all races have positions of leadership. (7) Back Catholic schools in minority neighborhoods. (8) Back legislation that fosters racial equality. (9) Keep the dream of a united world alive."[43]

In recent years, individual bishops have spoken openly and candidly about racial equality. In 2015 in a response to a series of incidents involving African American men and law enforcement officials that sparked national outcry and protests, Louisville archbishop Joseph E. Kurtz said:

> We mourn those tragic events in which African Americans and others have lost their lives in altercations with law enforcement officials.... In every instance, our prayer for every community is that of our Lord in Saint John's Gospel, "that they all may be one." ...

---

[42] The document specifically addresses the deaths of James Byrd and Amadou Diallo.

[43] National Conference of Catholic Bishops, *Love Thy Neighbor As Thyself*, 167.

We join our voices with civic and religious leaders in pledging to work for healing and reconciliation. Our efforts must address root causes of these conflicts. A violent, sorrowful history of racial injustice, accompanied by a lack of educational, employment and housing opportunities, has destroyed communities and broken down families, especially those who live in distressed urban communities.[44]

The Most Reverend Edward K. Braxton, bishop emeritus of the Diocese of Bellville and probably the most outspoken American prelate on race, made this insightful and powerful observation in a lecture given at the Catholic University of America in 2017:

We Catholics, like other Christians, sometimes have only a superficial cultural commitment to our faith. We do not experience our faith in Jesus Christ and his command to love at the deepest levels of our being. Only this deep existential commitment to follow Jesus as the Way, the Truth and the Life, will impel us to truly live the Catholic faith we profess in all of the complex and difficult situations of our lives, including those which will require us to oppose anyone and anything that serves to maintain the racial divide.[45]

In 2017, the United States Conference of Catholic Bishops established an ad hoc committee against racism.

---

[44] Archbishop Joseph E. Kurtz, Address to the Spring General Assembly of the United States Conference of Catholic Bishops (June 10, 2015), USCCB .org, http://www.usccb.org/news/2015/15-088.cfm.

[45] Edward K. Braxton, S.T.D., "The Horizon of Possibilities: 'The Catholic Church and the Racial Divide in the United States: Old Wounds Reopened'" (address given at the Catholic University of America, Washington, D.C., October 23, 2017), http://www.diobelle.org/our-bishop/writings/1133-the -horizon-of-possibilities-the-catholic-church-and-the-racial-divide-in-the -united-states-old-wounds-reopened.

The committee, initiated by Daniel Cardinal DiNardo of Galveston-Houston, "will focus on addressing the sin of racism in our society, and even in our Church, and the urgent need to come together as a society to find solutions".[46] Cardinal DiNardo noted that "racism continues to afflict our nation" and that "the establishment of this new ad hoc committee will be wholly dedicated to engaging the Church and our society to work together in unity to challenge the sin of racism, to listen to persons who are suffering under this sin, and to come together in the love of Christ to know one another as brothers and sisters."[47] The cardinal continued:

> Prejudice can lurk unnoticed in the soul. Without prayerful reflection, it can feed on the fear of what is different. It can grow into overt racism. But self-reflection is not enough. It must lead to action.... The vile chants of violence against African Americans and other people of color, the Jewish people, immigrants, and others offend our faith, but unite our resolve. Let us not allow the forces of hate to deny the intrinsic dignity of every human person. Let the nation and world see the one body of Christ move to the defense of our sisters and brothers who are threatened.[48]

In November 2018, the United States Conference of Catholic Bishops, through the Committee on Cultural Diversity in the Church, issued the pastoral letter *Open Wide Our Hearts: The Enduring Call to Love*. The document focuses on

---

[46] United States Conference of Catholic Bishops, "U.S. Bishops Establish New Ad Hoc Committee against Racism", USCCB.org, August 23, 2017, http://www.usccb.org/news/2017/17-149.cfm.

[47] Ibid.

[48] Ibid.

the sin of racism in society and the Church, and the urgent need for all of us to come together to find solutions.

> Racism arises when—either consciously or unconsciously—a person holds that his or her own race or ethnicity is superior, and therefore judges persons of other races or ethnicities as inferior and unworthy of equal regard.[49] When this conviction or attitude leads individuals or groups to exclude, ridicule, mistreat, or unjustly discriminate against persons on the basis of their race or ethnicity, it is sinful. Racist acts are sinful because they violate justice. They reveal a failure to acknowledge the human dignity of the persons offended, to recognize them as the neighbors Christ calls us to love (Mt. 22:39)....
>
> What is needed, and what we are calling for, is a genuine conversion of heart, a conversion that will compel change, and the reform of our institutions and society. Conversion is a long road to travel for the individual. Moving our nation to a full realization of the promise of liberty, equality, and justice *for all* is even more challenging. However, in Christ we can find the strength and the grace necessary to make that journey....

[49] There can be ambiguity here in how we think of racism and sin. People can wind up unconsciously holding racist attitudes as, for example, a result of social dynamics in one's family and upbringing or by thoughtlessly adopting the outlook of one's peers. Consequently, people may come to develop poorly formed consciences when it comes to how they think about race. Their wrong attitudes may or may not be things for which they are culpable, but nevertheless they hold what are objectionable ethical attitudes and, in that sense, sinful outlooks.

Whether people consciously or unconsciously hold such racist attitudes, they can lead people to act to "exclude, ridicule, mistreat, or unjustly discriminate against persons on the basis of their race or ethnicity". Such actions are sinful in themselves because they are unjust. Again, how culpable a person is with respect to such acts of racial injustice or how grave an injustice the acts themselves involve can vary.

It is important, as I note elsewhere, to distinguish between acts based on unconscious prejudice and deliberately racist acts. Racism involves grave sin when we choose to act unjustly on the basis of one's race or ethnicity, with full knowledge of what we are doing and with deliberate consent (see *CCC* 1857).

Love compels each of us to resist racism courageously. It requires us to reach out generously to the victims of this evil, to assist the conversion needed in those who still harbor racism, and to begin to change policies and structures that allow racism to persist. Overcoming racism is a demand of justice, but because Christian love transcends justice, the end of racism will mean that our community will bear fruit beyond simply the fair treatment of all.[50]

Open Wide Our Hearts is holistic in its approach and examines the issue of race from varying perspectives, taking into account theological, psychological, sociological, and economic realities. It even draws from hagiography, looking at men and women like Father Pierre-Jean de Smet, Saint Kateri Tekakwitha, and Saint Katherine Drexel, whose heroic virtue in the face of incredible obstacles both inspire and motivate us to follow their example. *Open Wide Our Hearts* is a clarion call in our time for all people of good will to work with dogged determination to break down walls of hatred and division.

The National Black Catholic Congress

In 1987, a year after the National Conference of Catholic Bishops established a standing committee for black Catholics, the Black Catholic Congress was reorganized as the National Black Catholic Congress (NBCC). The NBCC's mission is to establish an agenda for evangelization, to improve the spiritual, mental, and physical

---

[50] United States Conference of Catholic Bishops, Committee on Cultural Diversity in the Church, *Open Wide Our Hearts: The Enduring Call to Love; A Pastoral Letter against Racism* (Washington, D.C.: United States Conference of Catholic Bishops, 2018), 3, 7, 18 (emphasis in original), http://www.usccb.org /issues-and-action/human-life-and-dignity/racism/upload/open-wide-our -hearts.pdf.

conditions of African Americans, and to work toward the full participation of black Catholics in the Church and in society. During the ensuing decades and into the twenty-first century, the NBCC has addressed a number of issues of concern to African American Catholics, including strengthening family values, spiritual enrichment, support for Catholic schools in black communities, and, more recently, human trafficking, youth ministry, and faith formation.

According to their website, the NBCC's mission is based on the baptismal commitment to witness and proclaim the Good News of Jesus Christ. This commitment inspires us to

Enrich the Church by evangelizing African Americans within and outside the Church

Enhance the physical and spiritual well-being of African Americans as full members of the Church and society

Create an ongoing agenda for evangelizing African Americans

Collaborate with national Roman Catholic organizations.[51]

The NBCC holds a national congress every five years that renews and develops the NBCC mission with a pastoral plan. These national gatherings of black Catholics and those who minister within communities of color, and the pastoral plans that are generated therefrom, are outstanding examples and affirmations of the depth of cultural diversity within the Catholic Church. The congress attendees (myself included) have expressed joy and gratitude

[51] National Black Catholic Congress, "About Us", NBCCongress.org, 2022, https://nbccongress.org/about/.

at seeing so many people present who care deeply about serving God's family—of hearing both their aspirations and dreams, as well as their challenges and concerns, addressed and shared with like-minded brothers and sisters from all over the country.

The NBCC has also collaborated with other national black Catholic organizations in the furthering of its mission, including the National Black Catholic Apostolate for Life, the National Black Catholic Clergy Caucus, and the National Black Catholic Seminarians Association. These efforts have not gone unnoticed. Over the past several years, the Eternal Word Television Network has aired the annual convention of another NBCC affiliate, the Knights and Ladies of Peter Claver. All of these partnerships work to raise awareness of the many gifts and blessings that people of color are to the Church.

Final Thoughts

The Church's response to racism has been steadily making progress. The various pastoral responses by the bishops and the initiatives of lay organizations have brought greater awareness of racism to the American Catholic consciousness. Going forward, the emphasis must continue to be on the deepening understanding of the transformative power of God's merciful love, and its transition from conscious awareness, to interior acceptance, to lived action. This occurs first on the personal level where, in the midst of the busyness and distractions of life, care and concern for the dignity of every human person becomes a priority.

It is not enough to read documents and statements on race: the wisdom and knowledge imparted through the inspiration of the Holy Spirit must move from the mind to the heart, where one is personally convicted and motivated to love at the deepest level of his being. It is love that impels us to action, to become witnesses to society of a love poured out in service and self-sacrifice—to become balms of healing the wound of racial hatred and division. The Pontifical Council for Justice and Peace states it this way:

> *Discovering that they are loved by God, people come to understand their own transcendent dignity, they learn not to be satisfied with only themselves but to encounter their neighbour in a network of relationships that are ever more authentically human.* Men and women who are made "new" by the love of God are able to change the rules and the quality of relationships, transforming even social structures. They are people capable of bringing peace where there is conflict, of building and nurturing fraternal relationships where there is hatred, of seeking justice where there prevails the exploitation of man by man. Only love is capable of radically transforming the relationships that men maintain among themselves.[52]

---

[52] Pontifical Council for Justice and Peace, *Compendium of the Social Doctrine of the Church* (April 2, 2004), Introduction, no. 4 (emphasis in original), https:// www.vatican.va/roman_curia/pontifical_councils/justpeace/documents/rc _pc_justpeace_doc_20060526_compendio-dott-soc_en.html.

CHAPTER THREE

Critical Race Theory

Although critical race theory (CRT) includes the word "theory", it is more than an explanatory account of the phenomenon of race and racism; it includes as well a transformational and activist element. CRT scholars Richard Delgado and Jean Stefancic note that "the critical race theory movement is a collection of activists and scholars engaged in studying and transforming the relationship among race, racism, and power."[1]

Let us look first at the "theory" component. It is an intellectual hypothesis with the premise that race is not about categorical differentiation or biological distinction within a species, but a socially constructed instrument used to exploit and oppress people of color.

The origins of critical race theory can be traced back to the critical legal studies (CLS) movement, which, in turn, finds its origins in Marxist-influenced critical theory. The CLS movement examines "how the law and legal institutions serve the interests of the wealthy and powerful at the expense of the poor and marginalized".[2] Critical theory,

---

[1] Richard Delgado and Jean Stefancic, *Critical Race Theory: An Introduction*, 3rd ed. (New York: New York University Press, 2017), 3.

[2] *Encyclopaedia Britannica Online*, s.v. "critical race theory", accessed December 15, 2022, https://www.britannica.com/topic/critical-race-theory.

drawing from the thought of Karl Marx and Sigmund Freud, is a political philosophy geared toward the subversion of societal frameworks that are thought to dominate and oppress specific groups of people.

Critical theory is the offspring of a Marxist-inspired hybrid philosophy called dialectical materialism. Dialectical materialism combines the philosophy of Georg Hegel, systematizer of the dialectical process, with the Marxist philosophy of materialism. How, then, are dialectical materialism and critical race theory connected?

Gustav A. Wetter observes that "in Hegel's sense of the term, dialectic is a process in which a starting-point is negated, thereby setting up a second position opposed to it. This second position is in turn negated i.e., by negation of the negation, so as to reach a third position representing a synthesis of the two preceding, in which both are 'transcended,' i.e., abolished and at the same time preserved on a higher level of being. This third phase then figures in turn as the first step in a new dialectical process leading to a new synthesis, and so on."[3]

The foundation of the Hegelian dialectic is the constant progression of thesis–antithesis–synthesis. In other words, "dialectics sees change or process due to *conflict or struggle* as the only constant, and this *change and conflict* always lead to a more advanced level", according to the website All about Worldview.[4]

One can easily see why Karl Marx adopted the Hegelian dialectic and united it to his materialist worldview. For Marx, the process of evolution now operates not only in

[3] Gustav A. Wetter, *Dialectical Materialism* (Westport, Conn.: Greenwood Press, 1977), 4.

[4] Editorial Staff, "Marxist Philosophy and Dialectical Materialism", All AboutWorldview.org, June 16, 2021 (my emphasis), https://www.allabout worldview.org/marxist-philosophy-and-dialectical-materialism-faq.htm.

the realm of the scientific method and its accompanying disciplines of biology, chemistry, and physics but also in those disciplines rooted in qualitative analysis, such as philosophy, sociology, and politics.

Dialectical materialism is the basis of Karl Marx and Friedrich Engel's approach to transforming society where the thesis and antithesis of bourgeois (capitalist class) and proletariat (working class) give rise to the synthesis of Communism, whose "immediate aim", according to Marx, "is the same as that of all other proletarian parties: formation of the proletariat into a class, *overthrow* of the bourgeois supremacy, *conquest* of political power by the proletariat. The theoretical conclusions of the Communists ... merely express, in general terms, actual relations springing from an existing class struggle, from a historical movement going on under our very eyes."[5]

Subsequently, dialectical materialism serves as the foundation of not only critical theory but also moral relativism (the synthesis of essentialism[6] and nominalism[7]),

[5] Karl Marx and Friedrich Engels, "Proletarians and Communists", chap. 2 of *Manifesto of the Communist Party*, Selected Works, vol. 1 (Moscow: Progress Publishers, 1969) (my emphasis), https://www.marxists.org/archive/marx/works/1848/communist-manifesto/cho2.htm.

[6] Essentialism states that objects can be understood by discerning their essences. For example, if I say the word "dog", you form an image in your mind of what "dog" is and means irrespective of breed. As such, essences and natures are built into the very structures of the material world. The categories "dogness" or "humanness" are not metaphysical projections onto reality; we perceive them from reality because essences and natures are objectively present.

[7] Nominalism posits that material things cannot be known through the use of universal, abstract concepts but only by the empirical study of specific, individual objects. The differences perceived as absolute (e.g., the absolute difference between a rock, a tree, a dog, or a human) are, in reality, the rearrangement of meaningless moving particles. The "essence" and "being" of something, i.e., the idea of "humanness" or "dogness", does not exist in the natural world. What we perceive to be the "essence" or "nature" of something are simply external projections imposed on the human mind.

naturalism[8] (the synthesis of the scientific method and atheism), and critical race theory (the synthesis of radical feminism and critical legal studies[9]).

Critical race theory evolved in the 1970s as a response to what was taken to be an atrophied civil rights movement. The founders of the CRT movement include, among others, scholars Derrick Bell, Richard Delgado, Jean Stefancic, Angela Harris, and Kimberlé Crenshaw. They developed CRT as a way to examine history, national and cultural institutions, and societal structures through the lens of race. For critical race theorists, racism is not an exception in society but its *normal* state; it is woven into the fabric of the human experience. Racism, in the CRT model, is both innately individualistic and systemic.

Although not identical to Marxism, which assesses social conditions and hypothesizes that poverty (supposedly caused by capitalism) could be alleviated by revolutionizing power structures especially in connection with control of the means of production, critical race theorists similarly scrutinize hierarchical structures and assert that society's problems are due to intrinsically racist individuals and structures, and not merely the result of learned behavior of particular individuals that affect their attitudes, choices, and decisions. The goal, therefore, of the critical theorist is to "liberate" people from these "oppressive" structures through major societal and political change. CRT is, by its very nature, divisive, utilizing conflict, struggle, and

[8] Naturalism is the idea that the laws of nature, which govern the structure and behavior of the universe, operate in the universe and nothing exists beyond the observable natural universe.

[9] According to Delgado and Stefancic, "Critical race theory builds on the insights of two previous movements, critical legal studies and radical feminism, to both of which it owes a large debt." Delgado and Stefancic, *Critical Race Theory*, 5.

discord as sources of cultural revolution. Critical race theorists do not envision interracial collaboration as an anticipated outcome but, instead, foster the expansion of racial division as "progress" and "advancement". Delgado and Stefancic state it this way:

> Unlike some academic disciplines, critical race theory contains an activist dimension. It tries not only to understand our social situation but to change it, setting out not only to ascertain how society organizes itself along racial lines and hierarchies but to transform it for the better.[10]

Critical race theory has spawned numerous other critical theories, including lesbian, queer, and gender critical theories, critical feminist theory, and Latino, Asian, and Muslim critical theories as the continued progression of the thesis–antithesis–synthesis dialectic.

There are five basic tenets of critical race theory. I will state each principle individually and show why critical race theory is incompatible with Catholicism.

CRT tenet no. 1. Racism is ordinary, not "aberrational". This tenet states that racism is a "given" both within human nature and in American culture and is, consequently, the normal experience of most people of color.

As previously stated, critical race theory entails that racism is an inherent characteristic found equally within individuals and institutions. This assumes that the evil of racism is part of human nature, a position contradicted by Scripture:[11]

---

[10] Ibid., 8. "For the better" equates to the "advanced level" of the dialectical process rooted in conflict.

[11] According to Delgado and Stefancic, "Many critical race theorists and social scientists hold that racism is pervasive, systematic, and deeply ingrained. If we take this perspective, then no white member of society seems quite so innocent." Ibid., 91.

> Then God said, "Let us make man in our image, after our likeness." ... So God created man in his own image, in the image of God he created him; male and female he created them. And God blessed them.... And God saw everything that he had made, and behold, *it was very good.*[12]

This "goodness" in us comes from God and forms the foundation for the natural, moral law. The natural law is that part of God's eternal law (God's inner intelligibility) where human persons are able to discern the existence of God by reason alone. The heart of the natural law (synderesis) is the first general principle of the moral life: do good and avoid evil. Saint Paul puts it this way: "For what can be known about God is plain to them, because God has shown it to them. Ever since the creation of the world his invisible nature, namely, his eternal power and deity, has been clearly perceived in the things that have been made."[13] Likewise, "When Gentiles who have not the law do by nature what the law requires, they are a law to themselves, even though they do not have the law. They show that what the law requires is written on their hearts."[14]

Natural law, then, is not compatible with critical race theory since CRT disavows the existence of the natural law and surmises that racism is the "default setting" of human nature and society, and not the result of Original Sin (discussed in further detail below). At its core, CRT denies the possibility of divine wisdom working in the soul that elicits our cooperative free response through which humanity forms just societies by the implementation of positive (human) laws. As the *Catechism of the Catholic Church* teaches, "The natural law is *immutable* and permanent throughout the variations of history.... The

---

[12] Gen 1:26–28, 31; my emphasis.
[13] Rom 1:19–20.
[14] Rom 2:14–15.

rules that express it remain substantially valid. Even when it is rejected in its very principles, it cannot be destroyed or removed from the heart of man. It always rises again in the life of individuals and societies."[15]

Furthermore, God not only desires the creatures made in His image and likeness be aware *of* Him, but that they also respond to His invitation to intimate, life-giving communion *with* Him—to share in His life. This principle is stated beautifully by Pope John Paul II when he wrote that "God is love and in Himself He lives a mystery of personal loving communion. Creating the human race in His own image and continually keeping it in being, God *inscribed in the humanity of man and woman* the vocation, and thus the capacity and responsibility, of love and communion. Love is therefore *the fundamental and innate vocation of every human being.*"[16]

This relational dynamic is expressed beautifully throughout the Old Testament Scriptures in the invitation of God ("I will establish my covenant between me and you and your descendants after you throughout their generations for an everlasting covenant"[17]) and the response of His people ("You shall love the LORD your God with all your heart, and with all your soul, and with all your might"[18]). King David, the greatest king in the history of Israel and a man after God's own heart,[19] beautifully summarizes the nexus of natural law and relationship with God in the

[15] *Catechism of the Catholic Church*, no. 1958; emphasis in original. Hereafter cited as *CCC*.

[16] Pope John Paul II, Apostolic Exhortation on the Role of the Christian Family in the Modern World *Familiaris Consortio* (November 22, 1981), no. 11 (my emphasis), https://www.vatican.va/content/john-paul-ii/en/apost_exhortations/documents/hf_jp-ii_exh_19811122_familiaris-consortio.html.

[17] Gen 17:7. See also Ex 6:7; Lev 26:12; Jer 7:23; 11:4; 24:7; 30:22; 31:33; Ezek 11:20; 14:11; 34:24; 36:28; 37:27.

[18] Deut 6:5. See also Deut 11:18–19; Num 15:40.

[19] See 1 Sam 13:14; Acts 13:22.

Psalms: "He has put into my heart a marvelous love for the faithful ones who dwell in his land"[20] and "Your justice is eternal justice and your law is truth."[21]

"The first man," the *Catechism* states, "was not only created good, but was also established in friendship with his Creator and in harmony with himself and with the creation around him, in a state that would be surpassed only by the glory of the new creation in Christ."[22] Our Lord Jesus Christ, the fullness of God's self-revelation, came to establish the new and eternal covenant in His blood: "Do not think that I have come to abolish the law and the prophets; I have come not to abolish them but to fulfil them."[23] Quoting the Book of Jeremiah, the author of Hebrews beautifully illustrates how Christ is the embodiment of God's promised law from the Old Testament:

> "The days will come, says the Lord, when I will establish a new covenant with the house of Israel and with the house of Judah.... This is the covenant that I will make with the house of Israel after those days, says the Lord: I will put my laws into their minds, and write them on their hearts, and I will be their God, and they shall be my people."[24]

What is this covenant that Jesus came to bring? If we have the natural, moral law within us that teaches us to do the good and avoid what is evil, why did Jesus come to bring a new law?

The relationship that God established with man at the genesis of creation and invited him to share in was damaged

[20] Ps 16:3 in *The Liturgy of the Hours*, vol. 3, Ordinary Time, Weeks 1–17 (New York: Catholic Book Publishing, 1975), 823.

[21] Ps 119:142 in ibid., 1176.

[22] *CCC* 374.

[23] Mt 5:17.

[24] Heb 8:8, 10, quoting Jer 31:31, 33.

by Original Sin. Critical race theory contradicts the Church's teaching on Original Sin since critical theorists presume that the sin of racism is pre-programmed into human nature as such, failing to make the distinction between humanity's innate goodness and our fallen nature that inclines us to distorted and disordered behaviors that include the sin of racism. The first tenet of CRT says that racism is not aberrational but, in truth, that is *exactly* what racism is: an aberration resulting from the abuse of human freedom. We are not inherently racists. Racism flourishes when we decide to stop seeing clearly the image and likeness of God in the person standing in front of us.

In the Book of Genesis, our first parents were fashioned by God in a way that differentiates them from the rest of creation. Firstly, man was called to name all the animals and, as such, becomes aware of his superiority. "God blessed them, and God said to them, 'Be fruitful and multiply, and fill the earth and subdue it; and have dominion over the fish of the sea and over the birds of the air and over every living thing that moves upon the earth.' "[25]

Secondly, man is set apart from all other created beings by knowing that his personhood is communicated through the body; the body mediates and expresses the person. As Saint Paul taught to the Corinthians, "Do you not know that your body is a temple of the Holy Spirit within you, which you have from God? You are not your own; you were bought with a price. So glorify God in your body."[26]

Finally, man deepens his self-awareness by looking around and discovering that he has the gift of interiority and subjectivity that other creatures do not have, and his

[25] Gen 1:28. The Hebrew word for "subdue" (כָּבַשׁ) means "to bring under control".

[26] 1 Cor 6:19–20.

self-knowledge grows with his knowledge of the world. The more he sees of the external world, the more he recognizes how different he is from it and comes to understand that the loci of distinction lie within his unique, exclusive, and unrepeatable relationship with his Creator. The *Catechism of the Catholic Church* explains that "being in the image of God the human individual possesses the dignity of a person, who is not just something, but someone. He is capable of self-knowledge, of self-possession and of freely giving himself and entering into communion with other persons. And he is called by grace to a covenant with his Creator, to offer him a response of faith and love that no other creature can give."[27]

Hence, man is not part of the unconscious and "programmed" flow of nature, as critical race theorists would have us believe. Other creatures exhibit purely instinctual behavior while humanity stands juxtaposed in conscious awareness of our individuality and ability to choose freely. Saint John Paul the Great referred to this state as original solitude: man's inward, deep, personal presence to himself that cannot be penetrated by the created world.[28] In this way, God has engaged man personally in a covenantal relationship and made him a partner in the absolute. As the *Catechism* says, "The Church, interpreting the symbolism of biblical language in an authentic way, in the light of the New Testament and Tradition, teaches that our first parents, Adam and Eve, were constituted in an original 'state of holiness and justice' (cf. Council of Trent [1546]).

---

[27] *CCC* 357.

[28] For more on the concept of original solitude, see Pope John Paul II, "Meaning of Man's Original Solitude, General Audience of October 10, 1979", taken from *L'Osservatore Romano*, weekly edition in English, October 15, 1979, 14, https://www.ewtn.com/catholicism/library/meaning-of-mans-original -solitude-8510.

This grace of original holiness was 'to share in ... divine life' (cf. *Lumen Gentium*, no. 2)."[29]

Following the Genesis 2 Creation narrative, God imposes a limit that, at first, appears to curtail man's freedom: "You may freely eat of every tree of the garden; but of the tree of the knowledge of good and evil you shall not eat, for in the day that you eat of it you shall die."[30] This expresses the mode of man's freedom and self-determination, as well as his limits before God.

God gives man authority over the created world then directs his attention to the tree of the knowledge of good and evil. The tree is a physical reminder of God's authority and omniscience to which man must submit himself in loving obedience and trust. Not eating from the tree shows the honor, reverence, and respect owed to God. God initiated this limitation because He did not want man to use his freedom to renounce the communion of love he shares, thus cutting himself off from God's life and introducing sin into the world. Man's existence is a gift from God, and to disobey God does violence to that gift. Consequently, the sin of racism is not "normal" to human nature but, as with all sin, is the result of man's fallen nature—of man's freely chosen "no" to life with God.

All of this helps us to understand why God sent His only begotten Son to die for our sins and restore us to life with God.

We are all sinners in need of God's mercy, as Saint Paul reminds us: "All have sinned and fall short of the glory of God."[31] And as the Church teaches, "Sin sets itself against God's love for us and turns our hearts away from it."[32] In

[29] *CCC* 375.
[30] Gen 2:16–17.
[31] Rom 3:23.
[32] *CCC* 1850.

essence, sin separates us from God and the level of separation depends on the severity of the sinful act.

Sin is a weakness not a power, and it is only when we choose ourselves over God that sin has power over us. The light of truth reveals that the more we do what is good and pleasing in the sight of God, the freer we become. Conversely, the more we choose to participate in sinful acts that separate us from God, the more enslaved to sin we become. Death is the worst effect of Original Sin, and if we die in a state of unrepented mortal sin, then God will honor our free-willed decision to say no to Him forever, and we will inherit the state of eternal separation from God called hell.

This is why Jesus Christ became incarnate and died on the Cross: to free us, by His grace, from slavery to sin and the power of death. Racism will not be defeated by aligning ourselves with a theory that not only denies the inherent goodness of humanity but also relies on turmoil, struggle, and conflict to effect societal change. It is by freely cooperating with God's grace alive and active in our souls, and by aligning ourselves with Christ's teachings, witness, and lived example, that we can hope to overcome the tyranny of racism both in ourselves and within the culture. Saint Paul drives this point home magnificently in his Letter to the Romans:

> We know that our former man was crucified with him so that the sinful body might be destroyed, and we might no longer be enslaved to sin. For he who has died is freed from sin. But if we have died with Christ, we believe that we shall also live with him. For we know that Christ being raised from the dead will never die again; death no longer has dominion over him. The death he died he died to sin, once for all, but the life he lives he lives to God. So you also must consider yourselves dead to sin

and alive to God in Christ Jesus. Let not sin therefore reign in your mortal bodies, to make you obey their passions. Do not yield your members to sin as instruments of wickedness, but yield yourselves to God as men who have been brought from death to life, and your members to God as instruments of righteousness. For sin will have no dominion over you, since you are not under law but under grace.... But thanks be to God, that you who were once slaves of sin have become obedient from the heart to the standard of teaching to which you were committed, and, having been set free from sin, have become slaves of righteousness.... For the wages of sin is death, but the free gift of God is eternal life in Christ Jesus our Lord.[33]

CRT tenet no. 2. There are dual characteristics of "white-over-color ascendancy": ordinariness, and "interest convergence" or material determinism.[34]

Ordinariness, as defined by CRT, means "racism is difficult to address or cure because it is not acknowledged."[35] As a result, racial injustice becomes the commonplace (or "ordinary") experience of nonwhites. Although critical theorists do recognize that progress has been made regarding blatant forms of racism (such as redlining, immigration policies, and employment practices), they see these advancements as having no impact on so-called "natural" racism as articulated above.

To some extent, critical race theorists are correct in stating that some people do not acknowledge racism. The assertion that racism does not exist may come from a lack of direct, personal experience with racism or the achievement of a social status that brings with it a certain *je ne sais*

[33] Rom 6:6–14, 17–18, 23.
[34] Delgado and Stefancic, *Critical Race Theory*, 8–9.
[35] Ibid., 8.

pas quoi that presumably insulates one from racial injustice. Whatever the case, CRT's idea of ordinariness is, from a Catholic perspective, a position of hopelessness that denies the possibility of redemption.

Ordinariness assumes that everyone who is not a person of color is a racist, and the implementation of racist systems and structures within society is "business as usual". That might be true if humanity were not created for something more—for a purpose that transcends man-made ideologies. The Catholic vision of the world moves us from sin to holiness and virtue, and propels us toward our greatest good and ultimate end: life with God forever.

We must summon the courage to do what CRT does not want us to do: acknowledge that we are sinners and seek forgiveness. This recognition of our sinfulness before God comes through cooperation with grace— grace rooted in the virtue of fortitude, the Holy Spirit's gift of courage, and cooperation with the grace of the sacraments, particularly Confirmation. Humbly admitting our weakness before God is a challenging but necessary step forward in healing divisions. As I said in my book *Behold the Man*,

> Sin makes us uncomfortable. Sin embarrasses us. Sin opens deep wounds that are often painful. If talking about sin bothers us, then we should look at the Cross. Jesus took all of our sins upon Himself: He was uncomfortable; He was embarrassed; His body endured deep wounds that were painful. Jesus took our sins personally. He is the Lamb of God who takes away the sins of the world. There is nothing we can ever do, there is no sin too great, and there is no hurt too deep that cannot be forgiven by the rich mercy and healing power of God's life-giving love.[36]

[36] Deacon Harold Burke-Sivers, *Behold the Man: A Catholic Vision of Male Spirituality* (San Francisco: Ignatius Press, 2015), 67.

Next, we must seek forgiveness in God's never-ending wellspring of divine mercy. Divine mercy is a movement from the darkness of sin to the light of God's grace.

This is the depth of the love the Father has for us: that His Son endured the Cross, carrying the weight of our sins on His shoulders. In His human nature, where he suffered tremendously, Jesus was allowed to experience the feeling of alienation from God and endured death, the ultimate consequence of sin. But by His Resurrection, Christ has conquered sin; He has triumphed over death and has shattered the gates of hell.

The Paschal Mystery fills us with hope, a concept foreign to critical theorists. Connected to the natural law, as articulated in the *Catechism*, "the virtue of hope responds to the aspiration to happiness which God has placed in the heart of every man; it takes up the hopes that inspire men's activities and purifies them so as to order them to the Kingdom of heaven.... We can therefore hope in the glory of heaven promised by God to those who love him and his will."[37] The prophet Ezekiel wonderfully articulates how this grace-filled hope of heaven, rooted in our free cooperation with the transcendent law of God and not in the hopelessness of critical theories, opens us to a profound receptivity of God's grace while transforming us more and into His likeness:

> I will sprinkle clean water upon you, and you shall be clean from all your [iniquity], and from all your idols I will cleanse you. *A new heart I will give you*, and a new spirit I will put within you; and *I will take out of your flesh the heart of stone* and give you a heart of flesh. And *I will put my spirit within you*, and cause you to walk in my statutes and be careful to observe my ordinances.[38]

[37] *CCC* 1818, 1821.
[38] Ezek 36:25–27; my emphasis.

The *Catechism* goes on to say that "hope is the theological virtue by which we desire the kingdom of heaven and eternal life as our happiness, placing our trust in Christ's promises and *relying not on our own strength, but on the help of the grace of the Holy Spirit*."[39] The strength to overcome the darkness of sin lies in our willful cooperation with God's grace. CRT is an attempt to solve racism (or at least abate the effects of it) by changing systems, but the only way to deal effectively with racial injustice is by changing people's hearts, starting with our own. Hearts are changed when, in humility, they become open to God's loving mercy.

Christ's body was broken so that in His redemptive suffering we find healing from our own brokenness. Our Lord's most Sacred Heart was pierced, from which flowed His inexhaustible divine mercy, enabling us to become vehicles of mercy to others. In and through Christ's sacrificial death, humanity "attains to the merciful love of God ... to the extent that he himself is interiorly transformed in the spirit of that love towards his neighbor."[40] Jesus crucified hopelessness on the Cross.

CRT's assertion of humanity's inability to change punctuates the abject failure of CRT "ordinariness". In stark contrast, the Catholic faith professes a complementary and reciprocal truth: that in uniting our hearts to the graces won for us by Christ's death, we can extend mercy to others and, in doing so, experience mercy ourselves. "An act of merciful love," John Paul II says in *Dives in Misericordia*, "is only really such when we are deeply convinced at the moment that we perform it that we are at the same

[39] *CCC* 1817; my emphasis.
[40] Pope John Paul II, encyclical letter *Dives in Misericordia* (Rich in Mercy) (November 30, 1980), no. 14, https://www.vatican.va/content/john-paul-ii/en/encyclicals/documents/hf_jp-ii_enc_30111980_dives-in-misericordia.html#-27.

time receiving mercy from the people who are accepting it from us."[41] Hence, in a Christocentric vision of ameliorating race relations, "mercy becomes an indispensable element for *shaping* mutual relationships between people, in a spirit of deepest respect for what is human, and in a spirit of mutual brotherhood."[42]

The second pillar of "white-over-color ascendancy" is "interest convergence" or material determinism. Delgado and Stefancic explain that this aspect of CRT states that "because racism advances the interests of both elites (materially) and working-class whites (psychically), large segments of society have little incentive to eradicate it."[43] Material determinism, the continued expression of Marxist socialism, not only criticizes a faith-based approach to ending racism as idealistic and ineffective, but also characterizes legal advances thought to narrow the racial divide as naive, like the *Brown v. Board of Education* Supreme Court decision.

In this regard, critical theorists (most notably, Derrick Bell) surmise that the reason for positive legal advances for people of color during the 1950s and 1960s was to improve America's image among the international community, thus furthering its economic interests. Delgado and Stefancic note that "civil rights advances for blacks always seemed to coincide with changing economic conditions and the self-interest of white elites."[44] In other words, if there is a legal decision that supports racist ideology, whites win. If there is a legal decision that seeks to improve the situation of blacks, whites win. Subsequently, CRT positions itself—in true Marxist fashion—as the only possible remedy, the idyllic panacea of change.

[41] Ibid.
[42] Ibid.; my emphasis.
[43] Delgado and Stefancic, *Critical Race Theory*, 9.
[44] Ibid., 22. The full discussion occurs on pages 20–24.

"See to it that no one makes a prey of you by philosophy and empty deceit," writes Saint Paul, "according to human tradition, according to the elemental spirits of the universe, and not according to Christ."[45] Critical race theory is spreading among Catholics because we are not heeding Saint Paul's warning, succumbing instead to a so-called "woke" culture that embraces virtue signaling and rhetorical language as if they were revealed by God. We are hesitant to accept the obligations and responsibilities of faith with all that Jesus demands and expects of us. Rather, we choose to worry about being politically correct, being deplatformed on social media, or being "cancelled" by the culture.

CRT is a wake-up call for followers of Christ. In the story of the Tower of Babel, we see that when the people lived in loving obedience to God's holy will there was harmony, community, and peace.[46] But when they began to build their city and "a tower with its top in the heavens, and so make a name for [themselves]",[47] there was confusion, isolation, and discord. Critical race theorists, like the people of Babel, believe that trusting in a supernatural God is pointless because *they* are the creators of culture. Herein lies CRT's fatal flaw, which Catholics need to recognize: critical race theory focuses, to adapt John Paul II's words about the builders of the Tower of Babel, only on "the horizontal dimension of work and social life, forgetting the vertical dimension by which they would have been rooted in God ... and would have been directed toward him as the ultimate goal of their progress."[48]

[45] Col 2:8.

[46] Gen 11:1–9.

[47] Gen 11:4.

[48] Pope John Paul II, Post-Synodal Apostolic Exhortation on Reconciliation and Penance *Reconciliatio et Paenitentia* (December 2, 1984), no. 13, https://www.vatican.va/content/john-paul-ii/en/apost_exhortations/documents/hf_jp-ii_exh_02121984_reconciliatio-et-paenitentia.html.

CRT leads Catholics away from a faith rooted in Christ and centered in the Eucharist, and toward theories based on sociopolitical solipsism. Even faithful Catholics, who at times struggle with certain aspects of the faith, look for "new" ways to understand the world around them. We must be mindful that the methods and ideas promoted by critical race theory have nothing to do with Catholic teaching and, in fact, add to the confusion that helps widen divisions between people, fuel further misconceptions about the faith, and undermine Catholic identity. As Saint Paul observed, "The time is coming when people will not endure sound teaching, but having itching ears they will accumulate for themselves teachers to suit their own likings, and will turn away from listening to the truth and wander into myths. As for you, always be steady, endure suffering, do the work of an evangelist, fulfil your ministry."[49]

CRT tenet no. 3. Delgado and Stefancic note that the "social construction" thesis says that "race and races are products of social thought and relations. Not objective, inherent, or fixed, they correspond to no biological or genetic reality; rather, races are categories that society invents, manipulates, or retires when convenient."[50]

As stated previously, the definitions of "race" and "racism" are rich and complex, and are often conflated with other terms that are closely related to but do not actually meet the definition of "racism". CRT's narrow definition of race, limiting it to a social construct alone, simply denies reality.

Other contemporary black thinkers, like Ali "Hannibal X" Shakur, although philosophically similar to critical

---

[49] 2 Tim 4:3–5.
[50] Delgado and Stefancic, *Critical Race Theory*, 9.

race theorists in their Marxist ideology, offer a broader perspective:

> Racism has very little to do with race but everything to do with wealth and POWER. Racism is the cutting off of resources and opportunities to a group of people based upon race. When a white man calls you nigger, that is not racism, that is hate speech. If someone thinks you're a thug because of the way you're dressed, that's not racism, that's prejudice; pre-judging based upon appearances. When someone won't give you a job based upon race or the bank won't give you a loan based upon race or a school won't accept you based upon race, THAT is racism....
>
> Racism is a distraction. It was placed there to discourage one from reaching their goals. It's just another excuse for blacks to use when they can't hit their goals. In fact, racism is not as big of a problem as many make it out to be. The biggest problem we face today and have faced in almost every civilization is classism....
>
> What we are dealing with is rich vs poor. The have nots will almost always be oppressed by those who have.[51]

Critical race theory rejects one definition defined by *Merriam-Webster* we considered in the first chapter, that race can mean "any one of the groups that humans are often divided into based on physical traits regarded as common among people of shared ancestry" or that race can refer to "a group within a species that is distinguishable (as morphologically, genetically, or behaviorally) from others of the same species".[52] The major flaw of the "social construction" account of race and racism is that its

[51] Ali "Hannibal X" Shakur, "Racism and White Supremacy Does NOT Exist and Here's Why", February 22, 2016 (emphasis in original), Hannibal IsattheGate.com, http://hannibalisatthegate.com/racism-and-white-supremacy-does-not-exist/.

[52] *Merriam-Webster Online*, s.v. "race (*n.*)", accessed December 20, 2022, https://www.merriam-webster.com/dictionary/race.

consideration of humanity tends to look *outward* and not to look inward. CRT's theory does not adequately appreciate the fact that societies are comprised of fallible, sinful human persons, not simply structures and institutions. Sin is the eminent factor when someone believes in the superiority of his race over another. History shows that racism is based initially on wrong attitudes regarding differences in skin color, ethnicity, or some other biological or cultural element and that, when allowed to go uncorrected by the actions of God's grace and courageous people of faith, leads to perverted and abhorrent acts against the dignity of the human person, resulting in deep chasms within society. The *Holocaust Encyclopedia* recalls that

> the Nazi regime under Adolf Hitler aimed to purify the genetic makeup of the population through measures known as *racial hygiene* or *eugenics*. Scientists in the biomedical fields—especially anthropologists, psychiatrists, and geneticists, many of them medically trained experts—played a role in legitimizing these policies and helping to implement them. . . .
>
> When Nazi racial hygiene was implemented, the categories of persons and groups regarded as biologically threatening to the health of the nation were greatly expanded. These categories included Jews, Roma (Gypsies), people with physical and mental disabilities, and other minorities.
>
> Ultimately, Nazi racial hygiene policies culminated in the Holocaust. Under cover of World War II, and using the war as a pretext, Nazi racial hygiene was radicalized. There was a shift from controlling reproduction and marriage to eliminating persons regarded as biological threats.[53]

---

[53] *Holocaust Encyclopedia*, "Deadly Medicine: Creating the Master Race", United States Holocaust Memorial Museum, Washington, D.C., last edited October 27, 2020 (emphasis in original), https://encyclopedia.ushmm.org /content/en/article/deadly-medicine-creating-the-master-race.

The same "biologically superior" hermeneutic was utilized by famed eugenicist and racist Margaret Sanger, founder of Planned Parenthood. Sanger worked tirelessly to eliminate "human waste" that included those in minority communities and the disabled. As George Grant explains,

> Many Americans are unaware of Margaret Sanger's Negro Project. Sanger created this program in 1939, with the aim to restrict—many believe exterminate—the black population. Margaret Sanger aligned herself with the eugenicists whose ideology prevailed in the early 20th century. Eugenicists strongly espoused racial supremacy and "purity," particularly of the "Aryan" race. Eugenicists hoped to purify the bloodlines and improve the race by encouraging the "fit" to reproduce and the "unfit" to restrict their reproduction. They sought to contain the "inferior" races through segregation, sterilization, birth control and abortion. Sanger ... argued for birth control using the "scientifically verified" threat of poverty, sickness, racial tension and overpopulation as its background.[54]

Rather than "social construction", the Church would name it serious sin manifested as racial injustice at the cultural level of ethnocentricity. As the Pontifical Commission for Justice and Peace states,

> This is a very widespread attitude whereby a people has a natural tendency to defend its identity by denigrating that of others to the point that, at least symbolically, it refuses to recognize their full human quality. This behavior undoubtedly responds to an instinctive need to protect the values, beliefs and customs of one's own community which seem threatened by those of other communities. However, it is easy to see to what extremes such a feeling

---

[54] George Grant, *Grand Illusions: The Legacy of Planned Parenthood*, 2nd ed. (Franklin, Tenn.: Adroit Press, 1992), 95–96.

can lead if it is not purified and relativized through a reciprocal openness, thanks to objective information and mutual exchanges.[55]

The Church, recognizing the weakness of sin in persons and, subsequently, in systems developed and operated by people, gives the world hope moving forward rooted in the virtues and the human resolve to choose the good. The Pontifical Commission continues:

> The effort to overcome racism does in fact seem to have become an imperative which is broadly anchored in human consciences.... "Any doctrine of superiority based on the difference between races is scientifically false, morally condemnable and socially unjust and dangerous." The Church's doctrine affirms it with no less vigor all racist theories are contrary to Christian faith and love.... Everyone, therefore, must make efforts to heal it with great firmness and patience.[56]

CRT tenet no. 4. The concept of "intersectionality" or "antiessentialism" states that no individual can be sufficiently identified by membership in a single group, including race, gender, sexual identity, nationality, etc. Critical theorists closely identify "intersectionality" with "differential racialization" or "the idea that each race has its own origins and ever-evolving history", note Delgado and Stefancic.[57]

---

[55] Pontifical Commission for Justice and Peace, *The Church and Racism: Towards a More Fraternal Society* (November 3, 1988), no. 12, https://www.ewtn .com/catholicism/library/church-and-racism-towards-a-more-fraternal -society-2426. I will expand on the concept of "reciprocal openness" as a response to racism in a later chapter.

[56] Ibid., no. 33. Internal quotation is from the Preamble of the International Convention on the Elimination of All Forms of Racial Discrimination, no. 6; it was adopted on December 21, 1965, and entered into force on January 4, 1969.

[57] Delgado and Stefancic, *Critical Race Theory*, 10.

In other words, who I am as a person is determined by the amalgamation of personal lifestyle choice decisions, political alliances, religious affiliations, families of origin, or a host of other culturally determined influences. Delgado and Stefancic further note that the conclusion of CRT "intersectionality" is that "everyone has potentially *conflicting*, overlapping identities, loyalties, and allegiances."[58] For Christians, Jesus Christ is the heart and center of our lives, and He as God serves as the model for how we think, act, and live. Our faith is not a compilation of social constructs. As Saint Paul says, "I appeal to you therefore, brethren, by the mercies of God, to present your bodies as a living sacrifice, holy and acceptable to God, which is your spiritual worship. Do not be conformed to this world but be transformed by the renewal of your mind, that you may prove what is the will of God, what is good and acceptable and perfect."[59]

Interestingly, this aspect of CRT intersects with atheistic materialism.[60] The "self" becomes the autonomous arbiter of truth rooted in one's subjective experience and shaped by the process of evolution. As I stated above in relation to Marxist materialism—with striking similarity to critical race theory—atheistic materialism not only operates in the realm of rigorous adherence to the scientific method but also theorizes that relativistic moral choices are shaped by branches of scientific inquiry that rely on conjecture and qualitative analysis.

The popular material atheist Dr. Sam Harris summarizes this position perfectly and is worth quoting at some length:

---

[58] Ibid., 11; my emphasis. Again, we see the development of the Marxist idea of conflict as a path to change within CRT philosophy.

[59] Rom 12:1–2.

[60] See footnote 7 on nominalism.

When we look at the universe, all we see are patterns of events—just one thing follows another—and there's no corner of the universe that declares certain events to be good or evil, or right or wrong apart from us. I mean, our minds—we declare certain events to be better than others. But in doing that, it seems that we're merely projecting our own preferences and desires onto a reality that is intrinsically value-free. And where do our notions of right and wrong come from? Well clearly they've been drummed into us by evolution. They're the product of these apish urges and social emotions; and then they get modulated by culture. If you take sexual jealousy, for instance. This is an attitude that has been bred into us, over millions of years. Our ancestors were highly covetous of one another ... and this possessiveness now gets enshrined in various cultural institutions like the institution of marriage. So therefore, a statement like "It's wrong to cheat on one's spouse" seems a mere summation of these contingencies. It seems like it's an improvisation on the back of biology. It seems that from the point of view of science, it can't really be wrong to cheat on your spouse. This is just, just how apes like ourselves worry, when we learn to worry with words. . . .

So here's my argument, for moral truth in the context of science. Questions of right and wrong, and good and evil, depend upon minds. They depend upon the possibility of experience. Minds are natural phenomena. They depend upon the laws of nature in some way. Morality and human values, therefore, can be understood through science because in talking about these things, we are talking about all of the facts that influence the well-being of conscious creatures. In our case, we're talking about genetics, and neurobiology, and psychology, and sociology, and economics.[61]

[61] From Sam Harris and William Lane Craig, "The God Debate", April 12, 2011, Center for Philosophy of Religion, University of Notre Dame, Notre Dame, Ind., video, 33:14–39:01, https://www.youtube.com/watch?v=oAv_A-zJz1I.

The concept of "intersectionality" in critical race theory posits that one's individual moral compass can turn in any direction, and the tension and conflict of disparate human values are focused through the lens of gender identity, religious denomination, sexual orientation, level of education, personal preference, and on and on.

For Catholics, the "true" is a point of convergence where we meet Jesus daily at the intersection of His Cross, where the vertical beam (stipe) and horizontal beam (patibulum) meet. This is the intersection of life and death characterized by a life of sacrifice in imitation of Christ ("If any man would come after me, let him deny himself and take up his cross and follow me"[62]) and a life that never ends ("I am the resurrection and the life; he who believes in me, though he die, yet shall he live, and whoever lives and believes in me shall never die"[63]).

CRT focuses solely on the horizontal or earthly dimension of life with no reference to the objective truths that bind humanity together (the natural law) and, like atheism, completely ignores the vertical dimension (our life in God) that CRT proponents believe to be irrelevant and of no intrinsic value.

The CRT path of life always leads back to the individual, to the trinity of "me, myself, and I". In contrast, our Lord offers a radical perspective in Matthew's Gospel: "For whoever would save his life will lose it, and whoever loses his life for my sake will find it. For what will it profit a man, if he gains the whole world and forfeits his life?"[64] This is the question critical race theory's "intersectionality" and its promoters cannot begin to answer.

The martyrs who came before us, the great men and women of faith who died rather than deny Jesus, knew

[62] Mt 16:24; Mk 8:34; cf. Lk 9:23; 14:27.
[63] Jn 11:25–26.
[64] Mt 16:24–26; cf. Mk 8:35–36; Lk 9:24–25.

well that they were not giving their lives so that the teachings of Christ and the Church could be altered or manipulated by the culture; their deaths witnessed to the fact that Christ came to transform the culture with His truth. The societal attempts to reshape reality (e.g., the so-called "redefinition" of marriage, the transgender movement, and the "cancel" culture) do not define us. "Apish urges" do not define us. Psychology and physics do not define us.

In contrast to atheistic materialism and "antiessentialism" as determinants of moral choice, Saint John Paul II wrote:

Acting is morally good when the choices of freedom are *in conformity with man's true good* and thus express the voluntary ordering of the person towards his ultimate end: God himself, the supreme good in whom man finds his full and perfect happiness.... *Only the act in conformity with the good can be a path that leads to life.*

The rational ordering of the human act to the good in its truth and the voluntary pursuit of that good, known by reason, constitute morality. Hence human activity cannot be judged as morally good merely because it is a means for attaining one or another of its goals, or simply because the subject's intention is good. Activity is morally good when it attests to and expresses the voluntary ordering of the person to his ultimate end and the conformity of a concrete action with the human good as it is acknowledged in its truth by reason. If the object of the concrete action is not in harmony with the true good of the person, the choice of that action makes our will and ourselves morally evil, thus putting us in conflict with our ultimate end, the supreme good, God himself.[65]

[65] Pope John Paul II, encyclical letter *Veritatis Splendor* (The Splendor of Truth) (August 6, 1993), no. 72 (emphasis in original), https://www.vatican.va/content/john-paul-ii/en/encyclicals/documents/hf_jp-ii_enc_06081993_veritatis-splendor.html.

Jesus, in John's Gospel, provides the roadmap to true self-discovery in the gift of divinization, the indwelling of the Holy Spirit in our souls: "If you love me, you will keep my commandments. And I will ask the Father, and he will give you another Counselor, to be with you for ever, even the Spirit of truth, whom the world cannot receive, because it neither sees him nor knows him; you know him, for he dwells with you, and will be in you."[66] When we open ourselves deeply to God and neighbor in response to the gift of grace, we discover it is in giving ourselves away in love that we truly find ourselves in God. As the bishops of the Ukrainian Greek Catholic Church taught,

> In God's plan, the human person, created in the image of God, is appointed for eternal communion with the Creator. As St. Gregory of Nyssa says, "the purpose of a virtuous life is to become like God" (*On the Beatitudes*, 1). With the Lord's grace, a person reaches the height of its capabilities in likeness to God through "divinization" (*theosis*) (*Catechism of the UGCC*, Christ—Our Pascha, nos. 124, 127). The Apostle Paul describes the outlook and purpose of human growth: "... until we all attain to the unity of the faith and of the knowledge of the Son of God, to mature manhood, to the measure of the stature of the fullness of Christ" (Ephesians 4:13). Every human person in its growth toward the fullness of God's likeness is an absolutely unique and inimitable individual. This inimitableness is caused by the grace of the Holy Spirit, who endows each of us with special personal gifts, talents, abilities, and disposition. Thus, the equality of all people in their dignity is at the same time inextricably linked to the uniqueness of each human person.[67]

[66] Jn 14:15–17.

[67] Encyclical of the Synod of Bishops of the Major Archbishopric of Kyiv-Halych of the Ukrainian Greek Catholic Church concerning the Danger of Gender Ideology (December 1, 2016), no. 8, https://ugcc.fr/publications/official

When one's life is devoid of a moral center rooted in life-giving communion with God, we become slaves to our emotions and passions and succumb to the influences of our environment. This is why, as we have seen, CRT adopts the Marxist language of "conflict" and "struggle" instead of "reconciliation" and "healing" with regard to racial injustice. In the final analysis, "intersectionality" is a metaphysical car wreck.

CRT tenet no. 5. Delgado and Stefancic note that the "voice-of-color" thesis posits "that because of their different histories and experiences with oppression ... writers and thinkers [of color] may be able to communicate to their white counterparts matters that the whites are unlikely to know."[68] This makes those in "minority status" especially competent to discuss issues of race and racism.

There is definitely ground for agreement here. When my wife, Colleen (who is Irish and German), and I were first married, we went food shopping together at a local store. While she remained at the register to pay, I began wheeling the grocery-laden cart out of the store. Before reaching the exit, I was stopped by a store employee who informed me that "those groceries belong to her", pointing toward the register. I replied in an angry and annoyed tone, "You mean my wife? We're together!" When I told Colleen what happened, she was upset and could not understand why I was stopped. Not having my experience of being pulled-over for "driving while black" or being followed by store security in the mall, she could not appreciate what many people of color endure on a daily basis.

-documents-ugcc/encyclical-of-the-synod-of-bishops-of-the-major-arch bishopric-of-kyiv-halych-of-the-ukrainian-greek-catholic-church-concerning -the-danger-of-gender-ideology/.

[68] Delgado and Stefancic, *Critical Race Theory*, 11.

In essence, my experience as a person of color speaks a language that some white people cannot understand. So "minority status" does convey a certain proficiency in the arena of racial discourse.

That said, "minority status" does not convey exclusivity. Those who are not people of color, especially immigrants, also have experiences to share.

Legendary guitar player Eddie Van Halen, an immigrant from Holland, in response to a question about his first day of school in America, said,

> It was absolutely frightening.... You're in a whole country where you can't speak the language.... It was beyond frightening; I don't even know how to explain. But, you know, I think it made us stronger because you had to. I mean the school that we went to was still segregated at the time, believe it or not, and since we couldn't speak the language we were considered a minority. My first friends in America were black. Their names were Steven and Russell, and we became fast friends because I could outrun them [laughs]. It was actually the white people that were the bullies. They would tear up my homework papers, make me eat playground sand, all these things, and the black kids stuck-up for me.[69]

The "voice-of-color" thesis relies on the power of story to convey personal experiences about race. CRT correctly points out that there are many negative stories that convey myths and stereotypes, and not truth, about persons of color. The issue here is critical race theory's counter-narrative response: to tell the story of how the institutions

[69] From "Interview with Eddie Van Halen: Is Rock 'n' Roll All about Reinvention?", March 9, 2017, Smithsonian's National Museum of American History, Washington, D.C., video, 49:42–50:45, https://www.youtube.com/watch?v=yb26D8bBZB8.

and structures controlled by whites are used to marginalize people of color, particularly in the legal system. Acknowledging that standard systems of operation can tend to encourage sinful behaviors, CRT fails to appreciate the fact that sinful systems are comprised of sinful people, and effectively dealing with the immorality of racism can come only from first acknowledging personal evil and then working to change behaviors—to destroy barriers of hatred and create paths to peace.

Jesus accomplished this mainly using narrative and parables. "All this Jesus said to the crowds in parables; indeed he said nothing to them without a parable."[70] He did this to make the mysteries of God more accessible—to draw people *into* the mystery, into the very heart of God. The parable was not only an effective communication tool that Christ used to help the people visualize a concept, but His stories also powerfully connected listeners to the inner workings of God's mind and heart. Consider this short parable from Matthew's Gospel.

> The kingdom of heaven is like treasure hidden in a field, which a man found and covered up; then in his joy he goes and sells all that he has and buys that field. Again, the kingdom of heaven is like a merchant in search of fine pearls, who, on finding one pearl of great value, went and sold all that he had and bought it.[71]

Our Lord Jesus shows the people of Israel that genuine wisdom and knowledge, true happiness, and lasting peace comes when we seek God first above all else.

There is no question that some of Christ's teachings were challenging and, in some cases, difficult for people

[70] Mt 13:34.
[71] Mt 13:44–46.

to accept, but the goal was to preach truth that would lead the faithful from sin and death to reconciliation and eternal life.

Herein lies the weakness of the CRT concept of narrative: some of Jesus' teachings would be considered hate speech. Consider the following example from Mark's Gospel.

> And Pharisees came up and in order to test him asked, "Is it lawful for a man to divorce his wife?" He answered them, "What did Moses command you?" They said, "Moses allowed a man to write a certificate of divorce, and to put her away." But Jesus said to them, "For your hardness of heart he wrote you this commandment. But from the beginning of creation, 'God made them male and female.' 'For this reason a man shall leave his father and mother and be joined to his wife, and the two shall become one flesh.' So they are no longer two but one flesh. What therefore God has joined together, let not man put asunder." And in the house the disciples asked him again about this matter. And he said to them, "Whoever divorces his wife and marries another, commits adultery against her; and if she divorces her husband and marries another, she commits adultery."[72]

Jesus clearly teaches that matrimony is between a man and a woman as ordained by God since the creation of the world. Critical theorists would ignore this objective truth, opting to adopt the cultural narrative of "inclusion" and "diversity", redefining matrimony to fit their "antiessentialism" narrative. The institution of matrimony between one man and a woman, using CRT principles, is seen as a way to dominate and oppress individuals with same-sex attraction and must, therefore, be transcended by an

[72] Mk 10:2–11.

enlightened culture. And because this narrative has been enshrined in law, anyone who disagrees may lose his job, be deplatformed, "cancelled", or taken to court. CRT tolerates value positions that agree only with its ideology.

By CRT standards, Jesus would be labeled "close-minded" and "bigoted", as well as a "hater", for disagreeing with a personal lifestyle decision to attempt matrimony with someone of the same sex. But disagreement is not hatred. Refusing to drink the cultural Kool-Aid is not hatred. Speaking the truth in love is not hatred. As Pope Saint Paul VI wrote, "It is an outstanding manifestation of charity toward souls to omit nothing from the saving doctrine of Christ; but this must always be joined with tolerance and charity, as Christ Himself showed in His conversations and dealings with men. For when He came, not to judge, but to save the world, was He not bitterly severe toward sin, but patient and abounding in mercy toward sinners?"[73] This is the true Catholic counternarrative.

People of color telling their stories to empathetic listeners is an important and crucial step to healing racial discord. CRT is correct to state that the stories of marginalized individuals can help close the racism gap by inviting others into their experience. Our faith, however—following the example of Jesus—reminds us that these stories must move us to reconciliation and healing founded in truth, a truth that sets us free to love. As Pope Saint John Paul II taught,

A clear and forceful presentation of moral truth can never be separated from a profound and heartfelt respect, born of that patient and trusting love which man always needs along his moral journey, a journey frequently wearisome

[73] Pope Paul VI, Encyclical Letter on the Regulation of Birth *Humane Vitae* (July 25, 1968), no. 29, https://www.vatican.va/content/paul-vi/en/encyclicals /documents/hf_p-vi_enc_25071968_humanae-vitae.html.

on account of difficulties, weakness and painful situations. The Church can never renounce the "the principle of truth and consistency, whereby she does not agree to call good evil and evil good" (*Reconciliatio et Paenitentia*, no. 34)....

The Church's firmness in defending the universal and unchanging moral norms is not demeaning at all. Its only purpose is to serve man's true freedom. Because there can be no freedom apart from or in opposition to the truth, the categorical—unyielding and uncompromising—defence of the absolutely essential demands of man's personal dignity must be considered the way and the condition for the very existence of freedom.... Before the demands of morality we are all absolutely equal.[74]

[74] *Veritatis Splendor*, nos. 95–96.

CHAPTER FOUR

Liberation Theology

Some Catholics believe a theology of liberation, that is, a theological approach emphasizing socio-economic and political freedom from oppressive peoples, institutions, and structures, is a viable means of alleviating unjust inequity among the races. Similar to CRT, this approach to liberation theology tends to instill socialist principles into the discussion of race.

The widely acknowledged "godfather" of liberation theology in Catholic thought is Dominican Father Gustavo Gutiérrez of Lima, Peru. Father Gutiérrez, surveying the governmental and fiscal landscape of Latin America in the late 1960s, eschewed the term "development" (in the context of the "developing nations" of the Third World) that he believed was language used by oligarchies with strong international interests to increase their economic foothold in the region. For proponents of liberation theology, "development" was for those who oppress and dominate others in order to create social, political, economic, and cultural dependence.

Father Gutiérrez began using the term "liberation" in lieu of "development", explaining that "liberation ... seems to express better both the hopes of oppressed peoples and the fulness of a view in which man is seen not as a passive element, but as agent of history.... To see history as a process of man's liberation places the issue of desired social changes in a dynamic context."[1] Advocates of a theology of liberation consider political, historical, and theological aspects of "liberation" in the struggle for freedom from oppression and social disenfranchisement.

Those who support liberation theology propose that capitalism, by its very nature, creates great wealth for a few and great poverty for the majority who become the "oppressed" and "dominated". Looking through the lens of his Latin American experience, Father Gutiérrez sees capitalism as stunting the growth of nations and concludes that "there will be a true development for Latin America only through liberation from domination by capitalist countries."[2] How will this occur? By "a profound transformation" and "a social revolution" fueled by "a more or less Marxist inspiration ... through paths of violence."[3] What is the stated goal of liberation? To create a "society in which man will be free of every servitude and master of his own destiny".[4] In what amounts to a theological tagline, he adds,

> The word [liberation] and the idea behind it expresses the desire to get rid of the condition of dependence, but even more than that they underline the desire of the oppressed peoples to seize the reigns of their own destiny and shake free from the present servitude, as a symbol of freedom from sin provided by Christ. *This liberation will only be achieved by a thorough change of structures.* ... We are on the way to a *new conception* of unity and communion in the Church.... The Christian community['s] ... eschatological hope is that of *social revolution, where violence is present* in different ways.[5]

[1] Gustavo Gutiérrez, "Notes for a Theology of Liberation", *Theological Studies* 31, no. 2 (May 1970): 247.
[2] Ibid., 249–50.
[3] Ibid., 250.
[4] Ibid.
[5] Ibid., 252–53; my emphasis.

Finally, liberation theologians attempt to reconcile liberation theology and salvation history by arguing that "the struggle for a just society fits fully and rightfully into salvation history.... Christ thus appears as the savior who, by liberating us from sin, liberates us from the very root of social injustice."[6]

This brief overview of the basic tenets of liberation theology shows a clear connection to the principles of both critical race theory and Marxist ideology. I will now examine these ideas in more detail to discover if the utilization of liberation theology is an effective remedy to healing racial division. The areas for analysis will include revolution as modus operandi or praxis (including the use of violence), the incorporation of Marxism, and the eschatological approach to liberation and salvation history.

Revolution as Modus Operandi or Praxis

Liberation theology, as we have seen, is predicated on overthrowing despotic and oppressive regimes that prevent societies from flourishing socially, politically, economically, and culturally. Similar to CRT, the approach to liberation theology downplays the personal dimension of sin in favor of the social. As I pointed out in *Behold the Man*,

> Sin has both personal and social dimensions. Sin is personal because it is an individual abuse of freedom: the use of free will to intentionally alienate ourselves from God leads directly to sin. The willful act of sin, which can be influenced by both external and internal factors, "weakens man's will and clouds his intellect", and impairs man's reason and judgment, damaging the relationship with himself

[6] Ibid., 256–57.

and with God in the process. Sin is social in that the individual's sin has an effect on society and the whole human family. Social sin affects not only familial relationships but interpersonal and social relationships as well. This sin manifests itself through violations of basic human rights and privileges, and in the loss of dignity, honor, and freedom in all aspects of human life. From this perspective, we see that "the real responsibility lies with individuals", and so all reconciliation, penance, and *conversion must start with each man acknowledging his own sinfulness and turning back to God.*[7]

The razing of sinful structures and systems, including those that promote racism, can be fully realized only through a radical conversion of minds of hearts. This cannot be accomplished by deconstructing institutions through revolutionary action without, at least, a parallel process focused on creating a world of true freedom and liberation by identifying and rooting out slavery to sin. Since sin is an offense against God and a rupture of communion with Him (personal dimension), which at the same time damages communion with the Church (social dimension),[8] conquering all that separates us from God's love is the hermeneutic to which we must return over and over again when developing strategies to fight racial injustice. Catholics must work toward the authentic perception of each individual as someone created in the image and likeness of God and who, consequently, possesses human dignity and self-worth that must be respected by all. Unless solutions begin with this fundamental premise

[7] Deacon Harold Burke-Sivers, *Behold the Man: A Catholic Vision of Male Spirituality* (San Francisco: Ignatius Press, 2015), 61; emphasis added. Internal quotes are from Pope John Paul II, *Post-Synodal Apostolic Exhortation, Reconciliation and Penance* Reconciliatio et Paenitentia [December 2, 1984] (Boston: Pauline Books and Media, 1999), no. 16.

[8] See *CCC* 1440.

in mind—with emphasis on the recognition of personal sin as the precursor of social sin—nothing will change. As the Congregation for the Doctrine of the Faith stated,

> The full ambit of sin, whose first effect is to introduce disorder into the relationship between God and man, cannot be restricted to "social sin." The truth is that only a correct doctrine of sin will permit us to insist on the gravity of its social effects. Nor can one localize evil principally or uniquely in bad social, political, or economic "structures" as though all other evils came from them so that the creation of the "new man" would depend on the establishment of different economic and socio-political structures. To be sure, there are structures which are evil and which cause evil and which we must have the courage to change. Structures, whether they are good or bad, *are the result of man's actions and so are consequences more than causes.* The root of evil, then, lies in free and responsible persons *who have to be converted by the grace of Jesus Christ* in order to live and act as new creatures in the love of neighbor and in the effective search for justice, self-control, and the exercise of virtue.[9]

Liberation must be, first and foremost, interpreted through the light of the Gospel and the personal encounter with Jesus Christ, the Redeemer of man and the true arbiter of freedom. Jesus promises, "If you continue in my word, you are truly my disciples, and you will know the truth, and the truth will make you free."[10]

Humanity's deepest truth and identity is to love as God loves. Due to our fallen nature, we become frustrated

[9] Congregation for the Doctrine of the Faith, Instruction on Certain Aspects of the "Theology of Liberation" (August 6, 1984), IV, 14–15 (my emphasis), https://www.vatican.va/roman_curia/congregations/cfaith/documents/rc_con_cfaith_doc_19840806_theology-liberation_en.html.

[10] Jn 8:31–32.

when we cannot live according to this truth, and we come to the realization that we are finite and incomplete. Spiritual freedom comes when we willingly conform to the truth of who we are, to love with the love of Christ. Sin impedes our efforts to make this choice. It is in this way that sin is enslaving: it binds us to disordered love. The more sin becomes a habit, the more it fetters us to the fleeting goods of this world to which we have sordid attachments. Sin establishes an addictive pattern and keeps us from conforming to the truths of our being. Humanity's free choice needs to be set free, and it is Christ who accomplishes this. We need Christ's indwelling love to free us from the bondage of sin. "We love, because he first loved us."[11] Freely cooperating with God's love is our response to Christ's call to discipleship.

A disciple is one who hears, who accepts, and who carries out the teaching of Jesus in his life. A disciple follows and imitates Jesus. Living in the love of Christ is the foundation of discipleship. Discipleship is how followers of Jesus work to overcome the devastating effects of sin in the world. Each of us who has been baptized has this mission and calling: to share our experience of knowing Jesus Christ intimately (personal dimension) and then inviting others to share in His life (social dimension). This bi-dimensional discipleship must penetrate every aspect of the temporal sphere: political, social, and economic, where we live our faith boldly and unapologetically with a clear focus on the common good, from the simplest human interactions where we see the value of every person regardless of race, to a form of capitalism that creates opportunities for all to flourish, to the implementation of corporate policies that treat everyone fairly and justly. This is discipleship in action. This is how we end racism.

[11] 1 Jn 4:19.

Violence as Modus Operandi or Praxis

Liberation theology's modus operandi calls for the use of violence. According to Karl Marx and Friedrich Engels,

> The Communists disdain to conceal their views and aims. They openly declare that *their ends can be attained only by the forcible overthrow of all existing social conditions*. Let the ruling classes tremble at a Communistic revolution. The proletarians have nothing to lose but their chains. They have a world to win.[12]

The use of violence is an aspect of liberation theology that, even within its own circles, is highly controversial.[13] Since certain aspects of liberation theology link to elements of Marxism, which clearly advocates for violence as praxis, this issue must be addressed and the question must be answered: Is violence a legitimate method to heal racial conflict?

The emphasis on the need to liberate "systems" and "structures", with recourse to violence, presents a clear divergence from authentic Catholic teaching and practice, which should not be confused with licit civil disobedience. As the Second Vatican Council taught in its Pastoral Constitution on the Church in the Modern World *Gaudium et Spes*,

> Where citizens are oppressed by a public authority over-stepping its competence, they should not protest against those things which are objectively required for the common

[12] Karl Marx and Friedrich Engels, "Position of the Communists in Relation to the Various Existing Opposition Parties", chap. 4 of *Manifesto of the Communist Party*, Selected Works, vol. 1 (Moscow: Progress Publishers, 1969) (my emphasis), https://www.marxists.org/archive/marx/works/1848/communist-manifesto/cho4.htm.

[13] For an in-depth analysis of this controversy, see Frederick Sontag, "Liberation Theology and Its View of Political Violence", *Journal of Church and State* 31, no. 2 (1989): 269–86, http://www.jstor.org/stable/23916796.

good; but it is legitimate for them to defend their own rights and the rights of their fellow citizens against the abuse of this authority, *while keeping within those limits drawn by the natural law and the Gospels.*

According to the character of different peoples and their historic development, the political community can, however, adopt a variety of concrete solutions in its structures and the organization of public authority. For the benefit of the whole human family, *these solutions must always contribute to the formation of a type of man who will be cultivated, peace-loving and well-disposed towards all his fellow men.*[14]

The *Catechism of the Catholic Church* clarifies further, stating,

> The citizen is obliged in conscience not to follow the directives of civil authorities when they are contrary to the demands of the moral order, to the fundamental rights of persons or the teachings of the Gospel. *Refusing obedience* to civil authorities, when their demands are contrary to those of an upright conscience, finds its justification in the distinction between serving God and serving the political community. "Render therefore to Caesar the things that are Caesar's, and to God the things that are God's" (Matthew 22:21). "We must obey God rather than men" (Acts 5:29).[15]

> Armed *resistance* to oppression by political authority is not legitimate, unless all the following conditions are met: 1) there is certain, grave, and prolonged violation of fundamental rights; 2) all other means of redress have been exhausted; 3) such resistance will not provoke worse

---

[14] Vatican Council II, Pastoral Constitution on the Church in the Modern World *Gaudium et Spes* (December 7, 1965), no. 74 (my emphasis), https://www.vatican.va/archive/hist_councils/ii_vatican_council/documents/vat-ii_const_19651207_gaudium-et-spes_en.html.

[15] *CCC* 2242; emphasis in original.

disorders; 4) there is well-founded hope of success; and 5) it is impossible reasonably to foresee any better solution.[16]

For the Catholic Church, the "call-to-arms" is clearly not a proactive method to resolve conflict but only a *defensive* strategy when certain, specific conditions are simultaneously met. Utilizing the above criteria from the *Catechism*, liberation theology's violence advocacy does not meet criteria no. 2 and no. 5 since only the social dimension of sin is addressed, nor does it meet criteria no. 3 and no. 4 as evidenced by the tens of millions killed under Communist regimes in the former Soviet Union, China, and other countries.[17] The promulgation of violence also does not agree with the Gospel. "And behold, one of those who were with Jesus stretched out his hand and drew his sword, and struck the slave of the high priest, and cut off his ear. Then Jesus said to him, 'Put your sword back into its place; for all who take the sword will perish by the sword.' "[18]

Violence as a solution to racial injustice is futile. One of the greatest civil rights leaders who has ever lived, the Reverend Dr. Martin Luther King, Jr., understood this and advocated for a radically different approach than liberation theology. In his famous "Letter from Birmingham Jail", he wrote,

> It is unfortunate that demonstrations are taking place in Birmingham, but it is even more unfortunate that the city's white power structure left the Negro community with no alternative.

[16] *CCC* 2243; emphasis in original.

[17] See Matthew White, "The Black Chapter of Communism", in *The Great Big Book of Horrible Things: The Definitive Chronicle of History's 100 Worst Atrocities* (New York: W. W. Norton, 2011).

[18] Mt 26:51–52.

In any nonviolent campaign there are four basic steps: collection of the facts to determine whether injustices exist; negotiation; self-purification; and direct action....

As in so many past experiences, our hopes had been blasted, and the shadow of deep disappointment settled upon us. We had no alternative except to prepare for direct action, whereby we would present our very bodies as a means of laying our case before the conscience of the local and the national community. Mindful of the difficulties involved, we decided to undertake a process of self-purification. We began a series of workshops on nonviolence, and we repeatedly asked ourselves: "Are you able to accept blows without retaliating?" "Are you able to endure the ordeal of jail?" ... Knowing that a strong economic-withdrawal program would be the by product of direct action, we felt that this would be the best time to bring pressure to bear on the merchants for the needed change.[19]

What was at the heart of Dr. King's nonviolent approach? The example of Jesus.

Jesus' style of leadership and authority—the model of the Good Shepherd—is in stark contrast to a worldly culture that embraces a leadership model centered on power used to control and authority used to dominate. This secularized approach to leadership is exactly what liberation theology seeks to free people from, but instead of looking to the example of Christ as the primary solution to the world's ills, it seeks justice and solidarity using the same methodology as critical race theory: the radical conversion of social systems and structures.

There is a tendency in some areas of liberation theology to classify Jesus as a "radical reformer" who taught violence

[19] Martin Luther King, Jr., "Letter from Birmingham Jail", April 16, 1963, https://letterfromjail.com/.

as a way to facilitate change, citing the Lord's teaching that He came to bring "the sword" and not peace,[20] and in his action of overturning the moneychangers' and merchants' tables in the Temple.[21] However, did Jesus come to establish freedom from "systems and structures" in order to inaugurate an *earthly* kingdom, which seems to be the goal of liberation theology?

Let us first determine where Jesus' kingdom is located, then take a closer look at the passages from Matthew and Mark in context to see if Jesus was truly a "revolutionary".

Although there are passages in the Old Testament that record violent encounters, the prophecies of the Messiah's advent do not foretell the coming of a warrior-king who will reestablish the kingdom of God by violent uprisings and use of force. The Anointed One of God who saves, the Holy One of Israel, will shod His feet with the Gospel of peace. As the prophet Isaiah writes,

> Behold my servant, whom I uphold, my chosen, in whom my soul delights; I have put my Spirit upon him, he will bring forth justice to the nations. He will not cry or lift up his voice, or make it heard in the street; a bruised reed he will not break, and a dimly burning wick he will not quench; he will faithfully bring forth justice. He will not fail or be discouraged till he has established justice in the earth; and the islands wait for his law.[22]

The Messiah will gird His loins with truth. Isaiah continues,

> The Spirit of the Lord God is upon me, because the Lord has anointed me to bring *good tidings* to the afflicted; he has

[20] Mt 10:34.
[21] Mk 11:15.
[22] Is 42:1–4.

sent me to *bind up* the brokenhearted, to *proclaim* liberty to the captives, and the opening of the prison to those who are bound.[23]

The Messiah will be armed with the breastplate of righteousness and the bloodstained sword of the spirit. As the prophet Zechariah writes,

Rejoice greatly, O daughter of Zion! Shout aloud, O daughter of Jerusalem! Behold, your king comes to you; triumphant and victorious is he, *humble and riding on a donkey*, on a colt the foal of a donkey. I will cut off the chariot from Ephraim and the war horse from Jerusalem; and the battle bow shall be cut off, and *he shall command peace to the nations*; his dominion shall be from sea to sea, and from the River to the ends of the earth. As for you also, because of *the blood of my covenant with you, I will set your captives free* from the waterless pit.[24]

What does Jesus Himself say about the kingdom He came to establish?

Jesus answered, "My kingship is not of this world; if my kingship were of this world, my servants would fight, that I might not be handed over to the Jews; but my kingship is not from the world." Pilate said to him, "So you are a king?" Jesus answered, "You say that I am a king. For this I was born, and for this *I have come into the world, to bear witness to the truth*. Every one who is of the truth hears my voice."[25]

In my Father's house are many rooms; if it were not so, would I have told you that I go to prepare a place for you?

[23] Is 61:1; my emphasis.
[24] Zech 9:9–11; my emphasis.
[25] Jn 18:36–37; my emphasis.

And *when I go and prepare a place for you, I will come again and will take you to myself,* that where I am you may be also.[26]

Being asked by the Pharisees when the kingdom of God was coming, he answered them, "*The kingdom of God is not coming with signs to be observed; nor will they say, 'Behold, here it is!' or 'There!'* for behold, the kingdom of God is in your midst."[27]

Clearly, Jesus establishes that His kingdom is not earthly and becoming citizens in His heavenly kingdom must be our top priority. This is not achieved by a violent overthrow of earthly regimes since, as Saint Paul teaches, "The kingdom of God does not mean food and drink but righteousness and peace and joy in the Holy Spirit."[28] As mentioned above, we are called to be disciples and must work together as the Body of Christ to be instruments of Christ's peace in a world darkened by the sins of prejudice and racism. In cooperating with the grace of the sacraments, we acknowledge the power of the Holy Spirit alive and working within us, and we can come to a true appreciation of the liberating power of God's love that calls us not to hatred but to love. As Jesus Himself teaches in the Gospel of Matthew, "You have heard that it was said, 'You shall love your neighbor and hate your enemy.' But I say to you, Love your enemies and pray for those who persecute you.... You, therefore, must be perfect, as your heavenly Father is perfect."[29]

Let us turn our attention now to the passage from Matthew's Gospel where Jesus appears to be advocating violence as a mechanism for social change.

---

[26] Jn 14:2–3; my emphasis.
[27] Lk 17:20–21; my emphasis.
[28] Rom 14:17.
[29] Mt 5:43–44, 48.

Do not think that I have come to bring peace on earth; I have not come to bring peace, but a sword. For I have come to set a man against his father, and a daughter against her mother, and a daughter-in-law against her mother-in-law; and a man's foes will be those of his own household. He who loves father or mother more than me is not worthy of me; and he who loves son or daughter more than me is not worthy of me; and he who does not take his cross and follow me is not worthy of me. He who finds his life will lose it, and he who loses his life for my sake will find it.[30]

In Matthew 10:34, the "sword" that Jesus brings is objective truth. This truth divides the wheat from the chaff, the sheep from the goats, and even fathers from sons and mothers from daughters. This truth cuts away the chains of those enslaved by sin and leads us to spiritual freedom in God's holy will. As Monsignor Charles Pope notes, "The words shock, but they speak a truth that sets aside worldly notions of compromise and coexistence with evil. In order for there to be true peace, holiness, and victory over Satan, there must be distinction not equivocation, clarity not compromise.... Compromise and coexistence are not possible."[31]

Christ's transcendent sword of truth is not heteronomous—that is, His teaching is not something extrinsically forced upon us without any regard for our uniqueness as persons. This is not how love works. Rather, true liberation is built upon a participated theonomy that says the objective truth found in the natural law is designed for our total and complete happiness. This is a law that comes from God, and He desires that our inmost

[30] Mt 10:34–39.

[31] Monsignor Charles Pope, "Not Peace but the Sword", *Community in Mission* (blog), Archdiocese of Washington, July 12, 2020, https://blog.adw.org/2020/07/not-peace-but-the-sword/.

being willingly participates in this law, which corresponds with our nature and does not act against our free will. The sword of truth frees us to love as God loves. Hence, the sword Jesus wields does not cut through skin, bone, or corrupt earthy regimes, but through hardened hearts and obscured consciences.

Yet there are those who do not accept Christ's teachings, freely choosing to think and act like the world around them. They distort and pervert the Lord's precepts, conforming their minds to secular ideology instead of putting on the mind of Christ.[32] Jesus' teaching, however, is clear: "He who does not take his cross and follow me is not worthy of me." As Pope Saint John Paul II said in *Veritatis Splendor, "Human freedom and God's law meet and are called to intersect*, in the sense of man's free obedience to God and of God's completely gratuitous benevolence towards man.... Man's free obedience to God's law effectively implies that human reason and human will participate in God's wisdom and providence."[33] The active engagement and communion of our human will with God's holy will is how we effect deep and lasting change. This reality is something that liberation theology does not even come close to addressing, and, therefore, it cannot be considered a viable option to harmonize racial discord.

One last point that connects participated theonomy to the issue of race. There is no tension or opposition between individual freedom and a common, spiritual nature. Secular culture, which wants to divorce the two, says, "If I am really free, how can there be a common, spiritual nature that is binding?" As we have seen, within

[32] Cf. 1 Cor 2:16.

[33] Pope John Paul II, encyclical letter *Veritatis Splendor* (The Splendor of Truth) (August 6, 1993), no. 41 (emphasis in original), https://www.vatican.va/content/john-paul-ii/en/encyclicals/documents/hf_jp-ii_enc_06081993_veritatis-splendor.html.

the very nature of humanity itself is a universality that does not ignore the individuality and uniqueness of each person. A transcendent principle in the moral life says that every individual, regardless of race, possesses equal dignity. This can be known in its fullness by the truths of revelation, a portion of which (the natural law) can be known by reason alone.

The *Catechism of the Catholic Church* states, "By his reason, [the human person] is capable of understanding the order of things established by the Creator. By free will, he is capable of directing himself toward his true good. He finds his perfection 'in seeking and loving what is true and good' (*Gaudium et Spes*, no. 15)."[34] Consequently, willfully choosing to ignore the fundamental principle of synderesis—the innate orientation to do good and avoid evil—makes one culpable for one's actions.

This innate knowledge is clearly observable, for example, in the interaction of toddlers on a playground where the race and ethnicity of the other children is of no import. As I stated earlier, racism is *learned* behavior where people are *taught* to hate. I concede that it is possible that those who are the recipients of erroneous doctrine or exposed to external stimuli that engender stereotypes may, at the outset, harbor certain prejudices. Over time, however, and in cooperation with God's grace, ignorance regarding race can be tempered and even remediated through orthodox teaching directed toward proper conscience formation and lived experience gained from diverse social interaction. This fact does not detract from the truth that racism is a clear and deliberate violation of both the natural law and the teaching of Christ. One thing is for certain: the architects of hatred will be held accountable before God. For Jesus said to His disciples, "Temptations to sin are sure to come; but woe to him by

[34] CCC 1704.

whom they come! It would be better for him if a millstone were hung round his neck and he were cast into the sea, than that he should cause one of these little ones to sin."[35]

In Mark's Gospel, Jesus' cleansing of the Jerusalem Temple is another instance sometimes cited as indicating Jesus supported the use of violence to bring about social change.

> And they came to Jerusalem. And he entered the temple and began to drive out those who sold and those who bought in the temple, and he overturned the tables of the money-changers and the seats of those who sold pigeons; and he would not allow any one to carry anything through the temple. And he taught, and said to them, "Is it not written, 'My house shall be called a house of prayer for all the nations'? But you have made it a den of robbers."[36]

There is no denying that Jesus is angry in the above passage. What provoked this anger? Were the merchants and moneychangers oppressing or subjugating the worshippers? Were Jesus' actions a form of liberation? What's more, did Jesus contradict Himself? After all, He Himself taught "that every one who is angry with his brother shall be liable to judgment."[37]

To understand this passage in context, a distinction must be made between sinful and righteous anger. Anger, the *Catechism* says, is sinful when it "is a desire for revenge.... If anger reaches the point of a deliberate desire to kill or seriously wound a neighbor, it is gravely against charity; it is a mortal sin."[38] The *Catholic Dictionary* adds that righteous anger is "justifiable indignation. It is permissible and

---

[35] Lk 17:1–2.
[36] Mk 11:15–17; Jesus was quoting Is 56:7; cf. Jer 7:11.
[37] Mt 5:22.
[38] CCC 2302.

even laudable when accompanied by a reasonable desire to inflict justifiable punishment.... Such anger is allowable only if it tends to punish those who deserve punishment, according to the measure of their guilt, and with the sincere intention to redress what harm may have been done or to correct the wrongdoer."[39]

Clearly, Jesus' anger could not have been sinful since He is God and incapable of sinning. In addition, Jesus actions were not directed at the moneychangers and merchants themselves but their actions in the Temple. What were they doing that made Jesus so angry?

Jesus makes two references to the Old Testament during the Temple incident. The first is from the prophet Isaiah, who writes,

> And the foreigners who join themselves to the LORD, to minister to him, to love the name of the LORD, and to be his servants, every one who keeps the sabbath, and does not profane it, and holds fast my covenant—these I will bring to my holy mountain, and make them joyful in my house of prayer; *their burnt offerings and their sacrifices will be accepted on my altar; for my house shall be called a house of prayer for all peoples.*[40]

Pilgrims, both Hebrew and Gentile, made the journey every year to Jerusalem to worship in the Temple. Upon entering the Temple via the east gate, they arrived at the Court of the Gentiles, the place designated for non-Jewish worshippers. This was the outermost court which led to a series of inner courts (for women, men, priests) leading to the innermost sanctum, the Holy of Holies, where only the High Priest could enter. The Court of the Gentiles

---

[39] *Catholic Dictionary*, s.v. "Righteous Anger", CatholicCulture.org, accessed December 21, 2022, https://www.catholicculture.org/culture/library/dictionary/index.cfm?id=36101.

[40] Is 56:6–7; my emphasis.

was the area occupied by the merchants and moneychangers in Mark's Gospel.

The merchants were selling sacrificial animals (e.g., pigeons, sheep, and cattle) to pilgrims.[41] Jesus' issue with the merchants is not that they are selling animals per se, but that they were conducting their business in the court reserved for Gentiles to pray. In Jesus' mind, this is an insult to the Gentiles who could not offer themselves fully to God (hence his reference to Isaiah) since the true offering and sacrifice to the Lord is a humbled and contrite heart. As Jesus says in Matthew's Gospel, quoting Hosea 6:6, " 'I desire mercy, and not sacrifice'."[42]

Jesus' second scriptural reference to the Old Testament during the Temple incident is from the prophet Jeremiah:

> Behold, you trust in deceptive words to no avail. Will you steal, murder, commit adultery, swear falsely, burn incense to Baal, and go after other gods that you have not known, and then come and stand before me in this house, which is called by my name, and say, "We are delivered!"—only to go on doing all these abominations? Has this house, which is called by my name, become a den of robbers in your eyes? Behold, I myself have seen it, says the LORD.[43]

Since only Hebrew currency could be used in the Temple, the moneychangers were present to exchange Roman coinage for the Jewish equivalent, which was used to

[41] Jn 2:14–17 states, "In the temple he found those who were selling oxen and sheep and pigeons, and the money-changers at their business. And making a whip of cords, he drove them all, with the sheep and oxen, out of the temple; and he poured out the coins of the money-changers and overturned their tables. And he told those who sold the pigeons, 'Take these things away; you shall not make my Father's house a house of trade.' His disciples remembered that it was written, 'Zeal for your house will consume me.' "

[42] Mt 9:12. Hosea goes on to say that he desires "the knowledge of God, rather than burnt offerings".

[43] Jer 7:8–11.

purchase the animals used in the sacrifices and to pay the annual Temple tax. The problem is that the money-changers were artificially inflating the exchange rates and charging more than what was required for the tax. Their unjust and exploitative dealings with worshippers roused Jesus' righteous indignation.

The *Ignatius Catholic Study Bible* notes that "Jeremiah delivered a sermon of judgement to Israelites [who] presumed that the Temple guaranteed ... security and protection, despite their sinful living."[44] As a result, Solomon's Temple was destroyed. Thus, Jesus' actions serve a dual purpose. To cleanse the Temple of corruption and to establish the fact that, as Monsignor Charles Pope points out, "*He* is the temple. *He* is the priest. He is the lamb. It is His blood that will cleanse us. Temple worship is ended because what it pointed to (Jesus) is now here. Its purpose is fulfilled in Him."[45]

Jesus' actions in the Temple were not "revolutionary". Jesus' anger in driving out the moneychangers and merchants was out of honor, reverence, and respect for divine worship, and to establish Himself as the new Temple. In John's Gospel, "Jesus answered them, 'Destroy this temple, and in three days I will raise it up.' ... But he spoke of the temple of his body."[46] Jesus' directed anger was not "contrary to charity", because He did not act out of spite or hatred, nor did He "deliberately" desire "grave harm" to those he evicted from the Gentile court.[47]

---

[44] *Ignatius Catholic Study Bible: The New Testament; Revised Standard Version, Second Catholic Edition*, ed. Scott Hahn and Curtis Mitch (San Francisco: Ignatius Press, 2010), 44.

[45] Monsignor Charles Pope, "What Was the Lord Doing on Monday of Holy Week?", *Community in Mission* (blog), Archdiocese of Washington, March 29, 2021 (emphasis in original), https://blog.adw.org/2021/03/what-was-the-lord-doing-on-monday-of-holy-week/.

[46] Jn 2:19, 21.

[47] *CCC* 2303.

The Gospels, however, do mention the actions of a revolutionary who sought to overthrow the regime of his day. As Mark writes in his Gospel, "Now at the feast [Pilate] used to release for them one prisoner for whom they asked. And among the rebels in prison, who had committed murder in the insurrection, there was a man called Barabbas."[48] Jesus is not the poster child for liberation theology. Barabbas is.

The Incorporation of Marxism

As we have seen, elements of Marxist ideology are woven like a fine thread throughout the tapestry of liberation theology. So the question is this: Is the incorporation of Marxism helpful to the discussion of improving race relations?

Given the Cold War tensions at the time, in the late 1960s and early 1970s Marxism was a hot topic of discussion. Pope Saint Paul VI addressed Marxism in his apostolic letter commemorating the eightieth anniversary of Pope Leo XIII's *Rerum Novarum*. Regarding the alleged interconnectedness of Marxist ideology to Christianity, the Holy Father noted that

> while, through the concrete existing form of Marxism, one can distinguish these various aspects and the questions they pose for the reflection and activity of Christians [i.e., class struggle, political and economic power, socialism, and the scientific examination of social and political realities in history and practice], it would be *illusory and dangerous* to reach a point of forgetting the intimate link which radically binds them together, *to accept the elements of Marxist analysis without recognizing their relationships with*

[48] Mk 15:6–7.

ideology, and to enter into the practice of class struggle and its Marxist interpretations, *while failing to note the kind of totalitarian and violent society to which this process leads.*[49]

The pope was scanning the cultural horizon and saw that, in the wake of the Second Vatican Council, certain ideological schools of thought—particularly Marxism—were in a resurgence and possibly on an intercept course with the Catholic faith. The Holy Father was asking Catholic influencers (theologians in particular) to dissect these ideas so that their premises could be examined, critiqued, analyzed, and discerned before incorporating them into the theological disciplines of Catholicism. The Holy Father's cautious approach did not shy away from engaging these secular doctrines in contemporary dialogue. His goal was to filter the tenets of these renascent philosophies through the sieve of revelation to capture any ideas that were incompatible with the Christian conception of human dignity and the flourishing of a just society. This theme is echoed in the Second Vatican Council's document *Gaudium et Spes* when it states, "The Church, by reason of her role and competence, is not identified in any way with the political community nor bound to any political system. She is at once a sign and a safeguard of the transcendent character of the human person."[50]

As the years progressed, however, liberation theology continued to cherry-pick its way through Marxism, adapting the ideas of "class struggle", "oppressed classes", and "revolution" devoid of the empirical rigor called for by the Church. Consequently, the Vatican's Congregation

---

[49] Pope Paul VI, apostolic letter *Octogesima Adveniens* (May 14, 1971), no. 34 (my emphasis), https://www.vatican.va/content/paul-vi/en/apost_letters/documents/hf_p-vi_apl_19710514_octogesima-adveniens.html.

[50] *Gaudium et Spes*, no. 76.

for the Doctrine of the Faith intervened, issuing two documents less than twenty-four months apart: the 1984 Instruction on Certain Aspects of the "Theology of Liberation" and the 1986 Instruction on Christian Freedom and Liberation. In its Instruction on Certain Aspects of the "Theology of Liberation", the Congregation warned

> that atheism and the denial of the human person, his liberty and rights, are at the core of the Marxist theory. *This theory, then, contains errors which directly threaten the truths of the faith regarding the eternal destiny of individual persons.* Moreover, to attempt to integrate into theology an analysis whose criterion of interpretation depends on this atheistic conception is to involve oneself in terrible contradictions. What is more, this misunderstanding of the spiritual nature of the person leads to a total subordination of the person to the collectivity, and thus to the denial of the principles of a social and political life which is in keeping with human dignity.[51]

This statement, in a nutshell, is why Marxist-based liberation theology is not a good dialogue partner with racial reconciliation and healing. By employing Marxist thought with an uncritical eye, liberation theology fails to integrate the personal dimension of sin. As I have shown from a Catholic perspective, without the consideration of personal responsibility and an examination of the nature of sin rooted in objective truth, there can be no resolution to the race issue. The Congregation for the Doctrine of the Faith notes in its instruction on "Theology of Liberation" that "the ultimate and decisive criterion for truth can only be a criterion which is itself theological. It is only in the light of

---

[51] Congregation for the Doctrine of the Faith, Instruction on "Theology of Liberation", VII, 9; my emphasis.

faith, and what faith teaches us about the truth of man and the ultimate meaning of his destiny, that one can judge the validity or degree of validity of what other disciplines propose, often rather conjecturally, as being the truth about man, his history and destiny."[52]

The Eschatological Approach to Liberation and Salvation History

As part of his exploration of subthemes within liberation theology, Father Gutiérrez attempts to connect the concept of liberation with the redemptive work of Christ. "When we say that man realizes himself by continuing the act of creation through work, we are saying that he thereby places himself in the interior of salvation history.... It means participating fully in the salvific process that affects the whole man."[53]

Father Gutiérrez then examines several biblical texts (e.g., Is 32:17) to posit that this human participation in salvation history has a specific eschatological dimension, namely, that we are to assist the Lord in inaugurating a temporal kingdom of peace that presupposes the establishment of a just society. This just society is demonstrated by a rigorous "defense of the rights of the poor, punishment of the oppressor, [and] a life without fear of being enslaved".[54] He goes on to say that the eschatological promise carries with it "the power to change unjust social structures" and that the "end of misery and exploitation will indicate that the kingdom has come".[55]

---

[52] Ibid., VII, 10.
[53] Gutiérrez, "Notes for Theology of Liberation", 256.
[54] Ibid.
[55] Ibid.

There is an additional aspect of Father Gutiérrez's thought that should be considered. He says that this eschatological vision is truly fulfilled in "political theology". He sees the Second Vatican Council's document on the Church *Lumen Gentium* and its teaching on what Father Gutiérrez calls "the universal possibility of salvation" as a paradigm shift in the Church's ecclesiology that has eschatological implications. Father Gutiérrez continues,

> This shift in perspective implies a "decentralizing" of the Church, which is no longer the exclusive place for salvation, and now turns toward a new, radical service to mankind.... Political theology makes the Church "an institution of social criticism". This is a critique undertaken in function of its eschatological message ... to participate actively in constructing a just order.... But this eschatological perspective also permits us to grasp in a clear and dynamic way the antithesis: temporal vs. spiritual, and Church vs. world.[56]

Father Gutiérrez's first statement about human work as a participation in the salvific work of Christ while correct *on the surface* does not do exegetical justice to the deeper connection between work as a participation in the suffering of Christ and the full eschatological implication of that participation: sharing in Christ's victory over death. By placing liberation theology within the constraints of the temporal sphere, for example, overcoming oppression and demolishing social structures, the personal subjectivity of Christian anthropology and its eschatological fulfilment in the Paschal Mystery seem to lose emphasis.

The redemptive value of suffering is recognized in the Person of Jesus Himself. Suffering is most definitively

[56] Ibid., 259.

realized in the Passion of Christ and reaches its culmination on the Cross, where it becomes a source of love and self-gift. In the suffering of Christ, humanity enters the personalist dimension of sacrificial love: a love that embraces and perfects the good by means of suffering. It is in meeting Jesus on the Cross where humanity enters the paradox of redemption. It is precisely in the moment of our greatest pain and deepest despair that we reach the height of humility because our suffering has now found its deepest meaning in the transforming, redeeming suffering of Christ. As the Book of Hebrews says, "For it was fitting that he, for whom and by whom all things exist, in bringing many sons to glory, should make the pioneer of their salvation perfect through suffering."[57] Through the Cross, suffering itself becomes redeemed by God's grace that heals, elevates, and perfects our nature.

There is a profound and indissoluble link between sharing in the Cross of Christ and sharing in the kingdom of Christ. Human work after the Fall, especially the work of overcoming personal and social sin, means suffering with the Lord, and through this work we are brought closer to Christ (personal dimension) and the redemption of others (social dimension). The "glory" involved in our redemption is that the redeemed Christ is active in us, and the power of the Risen Lord enables us to suffer and to share in His Crucifixion, Passion, and death. As Paul says in Colossians, "I rejoice in my sufferings for your sake, and in my flesh I complete what is lacking in Christ's afflictions for the sake of his body, that is, the Church."[58]

Suffering means following and imitating Christ. Suffering for the sake of the kingdom has the power to convert people from sin and bring them to a higher degree of

[57] Heb 2:10.
[58] Col 1:24.

holiness and sanctity, and it is a key to overcoming racist and prejudiced attitudes within ourselves and in others. The hard work of conquering sin is not only temporal but has eschatological implications. When we suffer with Christ now, we know that we will one day share in His Resurrection. Suffering with and in Christ is suffering for the sake of manifesting God's kingdom. Pope John Paul II writes in *Salvifici Doloris*,

> To the prospect of the Kingdom of God is linked hope in that glory which has its beginning in the Cross of Christ. The Resurrection revealed this glory—eschatological glory—which, in the Cross of Christ, was completely obscured by the immensity of suffering. Those who share in the sufferings of Christ are also called, through their own sufferings, to share in *glory*.[59]

There is a sense of tension in the relationship between earthly and heavenly realities, as Saint Paul points out:

> For those who live according to the flesh set their minds on the things of the flesh, but those who live according to the Spirit set their minds on the things of the Spirit. To set the mind on the flesh is death, but to set the mind on the Spirit is life and peace. For the mind that is set on the flesh is hostile to God; it does not submit to God's law, indeed it cannot; and those who are in the flesh cannot please God. But you are not in the flesh, you are in the Spirit, if the Spirit of God dwells in you. Any one [*sic*] who does not have the Spirit of Christ does not belong to him. But if Christ is in you, although your bodies are dead because of sin, your spirits are alive because of righteousness.[60]

[59] Pope John Paul II, apostolic letter *Salvifici Doloris* (February 11, 1984), no. 22 (emphasis in original), https://www.vatican.va/content/john-paul-ii/en/apost_letters/1984/documents/hf_jp-ii_apl_11021984_salvifici-doloris.html.

[60] Rom 8:5–10.

"Flesh" (σάρκα) refers to "the things of the world; earthly things", while "Spirit" (πνεῦμα) refers to "the things of God; spiritual things". Paul is drawing attention to two disparate ways of living in the world: a life that is focused on what the world offers us juxtaposed to a life that God offers us. The effects of sin color the way we live in the world, so to focus on earthly existence leads to death; it results in cutting oneself off from the life of God. When we discard worldly habits and thinking, then the Spirit dwells in us and our attention becomes focused on spiritual things.

The tension, therefore, between temporal and spiritual is a matter of emphasis that has eschatological import: eternity with God forever (heaven) or being eternally removed from His love (hell). The temporal and spiritual conflict is not about achieving an even greater dialectical synthesis. The empirical battle flows from our interior resolve and free decision on how to live in the world, where the grace we receive from the liturgy and the sacraments strengthens and inspires us to cooperate with God's will ("the Spirit"), or we choose our will apart from God: a life of dissipation, carnal pleasure, and self-indulgence ("the flesh") taking our eyes off the Cross. As Saint Paul taught to the Galatians,

> Now the works of the flesh are plain: immorality, impurity, licentiousness, idolatry, sorcery, enmity, strife, jealousy, anger, selfishness, dissension, party spirit, envy, drunkenness, carousing, and the like. I warn you, as I warned you before, that those who do such things shall not inherit the kingdom of God. But the fruit of the Spirit is love, joy, peace, patience, kindness, goodness, faithfulness, gentleness, self-control; against such there is no law.[61]

---

[61] Gal 5:19–23.

We are "wired" to choose that true, good, and beautiful. A relationship of life-giving communion with God is what we were created for and what our hearts seek. "For," as Jesus says, "what does it profit a man, to gain the whole world and forfeit his life?"[62] The ultimate synthesis of "temporal vs. spiritual" and "Church vs. world" is not a temporal social order established by chaos and turmoil, but oneness with Christ, who, by the graces flowing from His death and Resurrection, unites all races and peoples to Himself. As the *Catechism* notes,

> He who believes in Christ becomes a son of God. This filial adoption transforms him by giving him the ability to follow the example of Christ. It makes him capable of acting rightly and doing good. In union with his Savior, the disciple attains the perfection of charity which is holiness. Having matured in grace, the moral life blossoms into eternal life in the glory of heaven.[63]

The bottom line is that the thesis-antithesis dialectic, driven by conflict and struggle as progressive instruments of worldly change, fits well into liberation theology's methodology but is unhelpful in bridging the racial divide that seeks integration and unity, not further separation. Overcoming racism must be a work of the Spirit with an eschatology directed toward heaven not earth.

Finally, Father Gutiérrez incorrectly interprets *Lumen Gentium* as teaching "the universal possibility of salvation" that leads to a "decentralizing" of the Church,[64] which is "no longer the exclusive place for salvation", thus opening the door for the Church to be a vehicle for political change.

---

[62] Mk 8:36.
[63] *CCC* 1709.
[64] Gutiérrez, "Notes for Theology of Liberation", 259.

Here is what *Lumen Gentium* actually says:

> Basing itself upon Sacred Scripture and Tradition, it teaches that *the Church ... is necessary for salvation. Christ,* present to us in His Body, which is the Church, *is the one Mediator and the unique way of salvation.* In explicit terms *He Himself affirmed the necessity of faith and baptism and thereby affirmed also the necessity of the Church....* Whosoever, therefore, knowing that the Catholic Church was made necessary by Christ, would refuse to enter or to remain in it, could not be saved.[65]

Referring specifically to "those who have not yet received the Gospel are related in various ways to the people of God", it adds:

> Those also can attain to salvation who *through no fault of their own* do not know the Gospel of Christ or His Church, yet sincerely seek God and moved by grace strive by their deeds to do His will as it is known to them through the dictates of conscience. Nor does Divine Providence deny the helps necessary for salvation to those who, *without blame on their part,* have not yet arrived at an explicit knowledge of God and with His grace strive to live a good life. Whatever good or truth is found amongst them is looked upon by the Church as a preparation for the Gospel.[66]

The Second Vatican Council clearly states the Church, echoing Christ, is necessary for salvation, yet speaks of the *possibility* of salvation outside of the *visible boundaries*

---

[65] Vatican Council II, Dogmatic Constitution on the Church *Lumen Gentium* (November 21, 1964), no. 14 (my emphasis), https://www.vatican.va/archive /hist_councils/ii_vatican_council/documents/vat-ii_const_19641121 _lumen-gentium_en.html.

[66] Ibid., no. 16; my emphasis.

of the Church for a specified group of people under certain conditions *when* they follow the natural moral law. Conversely, Father Gutiérrez, in omitting the qualifications given in *Lumen Gentium* above, incorrectly concludes that (1) *Lumen Gentium* implied universal salvation for all per se, and (2) the Church is now an institution for social criticism and political revolution.

The Church is not a political organization, but the Church recognizes mankind's legitimate earthly authority as part of God's divine plan. As Saint Paul says to the Romans, "Let every person be subject to the governing authorities. For there is no authority except from God, and those that exist have been instituted by God. Therefore he who resists the authorities resists what God has appointed, and those who resist will incur judgment."[67] The Second Vatican Council in *Gaudium et Spes* adds, "It follows also that political authority ... must always be exercised within the limits of the moral order and directed toward the common good ... according to the juridical order legitimately established or due to be established. When authority is so exercised, citizens are bound in conscience to obey."[68]

Legitimate political authority is not exercised by clerics or the Magisterium of the Church.[69] Authority in the political realm clearly falls to the laity who hold political office and ensure that temporal affairs are ordered toward the common good. Political authority in a pluralistic

[67] Rom 13:1–2.

[68] *Gaudium et Spes*, no. 74.

[69] According to canon law, "Clerics are forbidden to assume public offices which entail a participation in the exercise of civil power. Without the permission of their ordinary, they are not to take on the management of goods belonging to lay persons or secular offices which entail an obligation of rendering accounts." *Code of Canon Law, New English Translation* (Washington, D.C.: Libreria Editrice Vaticana—Canon Law Society of America, 1989), can. 285 §§3–4.

society is not exercised in the name of the Church. Catholic politicians, guided by the dictates of a well-formed conscience, should enact positive laws that have their point of reference in the natural law. This means that, as Pope John Paul II states in *Evangelium Vitae*, "the dignity of every human person, respect for inviolable and inalienable human rights, and the adoption of the 'common good' as the end and criterion regulating political life are certainly fundamental and not to be ignored"[70] when promulgating civil laws.

The life of a Christian politician comes with grave personal responsibilities that must not be taken lightly. No politician, the Holy Father continues, "can ever renounce this responsibility, especially when he or she has a legislative or decision-making mandate, which calls that person to answer to God, to his or her own conscience, and the whole of society for choices which may be contrary to the common good."[71]

Father Gutiérrez is correct that the Church can be a vehicle for political change, but since he does not specify the "Church" as laity properly exercising their authority in the temporal sphere of politics, it may be misconstrued that clerics or the Magisterium are the enactors of political revolution. As the Second Vatican Council stated in *Gaudium et Spes*, "The Church and the political community in their own fields are autonomous and independent from each other.... The Church, by reason of her role and competence, is not identified in any way with the political community nor bound to any political system. She is at once a sign and a safeguard of the transcendent character of

---

[70] Pope John Paul II, encyclical letter *Evangelium Vitae* (Gospel of Life) (March 25, 1995), no. 70, https://www.vatican.va/content/john-paul-ii/en/encyclicals/documents/hf_jp-ii_enc_25031995_evangelium-vitae.html.

[71] Ibid., no. 90.

the human person. The Church ... does not place her trust in the privileges offered by civil authority."[72]

The Church, in bridging the chasm of racial division in the political realm, takes a two-pronged approach that does not rely on social revolution, violence, Marxism, political theology, and decentralization to accomplish her task. The teaching authority of the Church helps laity form their consciences according to the true and the good flowing from the divine law revealed by Christ. The lay faithful, through the judgment of conscience and the exercise of prudence, incorporate divine truth and goodness into the temporal world of politics. The Church (Magisterium and laity) works together to overcome the darkness of sin that obscures the vision of racial unity so that, through human law, the love of God may shine brightly, manifesting itself in virtue so that the world may see the good works that we do and give glory to the Father in heaven.[73] The Church teaches in the Vatican II document *Gaudium et Spes*,

It does [government officials] no good to work for peace as long as feelings of hostility, contempt and distrust, as well as racial hatred and unbending ideologies, continue to divide men and place them in opposing camps. Consequently there is above all a pressing need for a renewed education of attitudes and for new inspiration in public opinion. Those who ... mold public opinion, should consider it their most weighty task to instruct all in fresh sentiments of peace. Indeed, we all need a change of heart as we regard the entire world and those tasks which we can perform in unison for the betterment of our race.[74]

[72] *Gaudium et Spes*, no. 76.
[73] Cf. Mt 5:16.
[74] *Gaudium et Spes*, no. 82.

It is the Church's responsibility to form minds and hearts according to the dictates of the natural law and the teachings of Jesus Christ. The Church, working together with lay politicians, helps to guarantee that the God-given rights of every human person, ordered to the good of all, are safeguarded and treasured so that through these efforts, rooted in the Gospel, all people of good will may come to experience the love of God, increase their desire to know Him more fully, and long for everlasting life with Him in heaven.

Black Liberation Theology[75]

The period between the mid-1800s and the early 1950s saw the rise of the black liberation movement from which emerged black liberation theology. Protestant theologian Ron Rhodes notes:

> Beginning with the "black power" movement in 1966, black clergy in many major denominations began to reassess the relationship of the Christian church to the black community....
>
> Black clergy ... and black theologians began to recognize the need for a completely new "starting point" in theology. They insisted that this starting point be defined by people at the bottom and not the top of the socioeconomic ladder. So, black theologians began to re-read the bible through the eyes of their slave grandparents and started to speak of God's solidarity with the oppressed of the earth.[76]

---

[75] This section is an expansion of part of a chapter from my previous book *Father Augustus Tolton: The Slave Who Became the First African-American Priest* (Irondale, Ala.: EWTN Publishing, 2018), 129–33.

[76] Ron Rhodes, "Black Theology, Black Power, and the Black Experience", under "The Emergence of a Formal 'Black Theology'", Reasoning from the Scriptures Ministries, 2022, https://www.ronrhodes.org/black-theology-black-power-and-the-bla.

This effort was led by Protestant theologian Dr. James H. Cone in his seminal work *A Black Theology of Liberation*, where he outlines the task of black liberation theology. He states,

> It is *a rational study of the being of God in the world in light of the existential situation of an oppressed community, relating the forces of liberation to the essence of the gospel, which is Jesus Christ.* . . . There can be no Christian theology which is not identified unreservedly with those who are humiliated and abused. . . . The task of theology then is to explicate the meaning of God's liberating activity so that those who labor under enslaving powers will see that the forces of liberation are the activity of God himself. . . . The task of theology, then, is to analyze the meaning of hope in God in such a way that the oppressed community of a given society will risk all for earthly freedom.[77]

Cone states that black liberation theology arises out of the biblical tradition, specifically, Israel's experience of slavery in the Old Testament Book of Exodus, and Jesus' condemnation of the rich and His emphasis on the poor in the New Testament. Cone says, "To suggest that [Jesus] was speaking of a 'spiritual' liberation fails to take seriously Jesus' thoroughly Hebrew view of man . . . that has far-reaching implications for economic, political, and social institutions."[78] Not surprisingly, Cone echoes familiar themes found in both critical race theory and liberation theology.

Cone's point of departure lies within the juxtaposition of what he calls "white theology" and "black theology". He describes white theology as the theology of the oppressor that ignores black suffering and identifies with white

---

[77] James H. Cone, *A Black Theology of Liberation* (New York: J. B. Lippincott, 1970), 17, 20–21; emphasis in original.
[78] Ibid., 20.

racism "that can only mean death to black people".[79] Cone defines black theology as a synthesis of the Gospel "in light of oppressed black people so they will see the gospel as inseparable from their humiliated condition, bestowing on them the necessary power to break the chains of oppression ... by whatever means they regard as suitable."[80]

Interestingly, Cone does not limit black liberation theology to black people since being black "stands for all victims of oppression who realize that their humanity is inseparable from man's liberation from whiteness".[81] But he does not stop there. In language that can be described only as highly polemical and triumphalist, Cone says that, insofar as the United States is trying to make whiteness the dominant power in the world, "whiteness is the symbol for the Antichrist" and by analyzing "the satanic nature of whiteness", nonwhites can adequately prepare for revolutionary action.[82] Like CRT and liberation theology, tension, conflict, struggle, and revolution are hallmarks in black liberation theology.

Dr. Cone also offers a contemporary interpretation of divine revelation envisaged through the lens of black liberation theology.

> In the New Testament, the revelatory event of God takes place in the person of Christ. He is the event of God, telling us who God is ... he is the complete revelation of God.... The weakness of white American theology is that it seldom gets beyond the first century in its analysis of revelation.... For black theology, revelation is not *just* a past event.... *Revelation is a black event, i.e.,* what black

[79] Ibid., 22.
[80] Ibid., 23–24.
[81] Ibid., 28.
[82] Ibid., 29.

people are doing about their liberation.... According to Black Theology, revelation must mean more than just divine self-disclosure. Revelation is God's self-disclosure to man *in a situation of liberation*.... God's revelation means liberation, an emancipation from the political, economic and social structures of the society. This is the essence of the biblical revelation.[83]

Finally, Dr. Cone takes a unique perspective on human freedom and the nature of sin.

> Freedom means an affirmation of blackness. To be free is to be black.... The free man in America is the man who does not tolerate whiteness but fights against it, knowing that is the source of human misery.... Being free in America means accepting blackness as the only possible way of existing in the world.... It means rejecting white proposals for peace and reconciliation....
>
> Sin is an alienation from the source of humanity in the world, resulting in human oppression and misery... There can be no knowledge of the sinful condition except in the movement of an oppressed community claiming its freedom. This means that white people ... are rendered incapable of making valid judgements on the character of sin.... What we need is the destruction of whiteness, which is the source of human misery in the world.... In a word, sin is whiteness—white people's desire to be God in human relations.[84]

It is extremely difficult, if not impossible, to see how Cone's presentation of black liberation theology can be a source and catalyst for reconciliation and healing between the races.

---

[83] Ibid., 64–65, 91; emphasis in original.
[84] Ibid., 183, 190–93.

Dr. Cone's understanding of Jesus Christ as the fullness of God's divine self-disclosure to humanity is spot-on. The *Catechism of the Catholic Church* says that revelation "has not been made completely explicit; it remains for Christian faith gradually to grasp its full significance over the course of the centuries";[85] Cone's attempt to comingle revelation with black theology in a way that creates a "situation of liberation" does not explicate but actually constricts the vision of revelation, reducing its temporal fulfillment within the new and everlasting covenant of the Christian economy to a rallying cry for marginalized and oppressed people. Dr. Cone's approach is devoid of an anagogical sense of eternity but rather, as we have seen with liberation theology, has an emphatically earthy emphasis: the "emancipation from the political, economic and social structures of the society". This is not, as Dr. Cone claims, the "essence of biblical revelation" since, as the Second Vatican Council articulates in *Dei Verbum*, "through divine revelation, God chose to show forth and communicate Himself and the *eternal* decisions of His will regarding the salvation of men. That is to say, He chose to share with them those divine treasures which *totally transcend the understanding of the human mind.*"[86]

Cone's anthropology of sin and human freedom as it relates to a theology of liberation seems to have no doctrinal basis but is simply an *ad hominem* attack against white people. The Gospel is color blind. In the Lord's Prayer, Jesus teaches us that the Father in heaven will forgive us to the extent that we forgive others: "For if you forgive men their trespasses, your heavenly Father also will

[85] *CCC* 66.

[86] Vatican Council II, Dogmatic Constitution on Divine Revelation *Dei Verbum* (November 18, 1965), no. 6 (my emphasis), https://www.vatican.va/archive/hist_councils/ii_vatican_council/documents/vat-ii_const_19651118_dei-verbum_en.html.

forgive you; but if you do not forgive men their trespasses, neither will your Father forgive your trespasses."[87]
We must ensure that systems are in place so that the errors
of the past are not repeated, but we must also work diligently to build a culture of forgiveness and reconciliation,
two hallmarks of Christ's earthy ministry. The *Catechism
of the Catholic Church* reminds us of this fact when it says,
"During his public life Jesus not only forgave sins, but also
made plain the effect of this forgiveness: he reintegrated
forgiven sinners into the community of the People of God
from which sin had alienated or even excluded them. A
remarkable sign of this is the fact that Jesus receives sinners at his table, a gesture that expresses in an astonishing
way both God's forgiveness and the return to the bosom
of the People of God."[88]

There are several theologians of color, most notably Dr. Diana L. Hayes, Dr. Jamie T. Phelps, O.P., and
Dr. M. Shawn Copeland, who have adapted black liberation theology to a Catholic context. Black Catholic
theologians took a more holistic approach to the topic,
linking the centuries-old black experience of segregation
and discrimination—along with the struggle for freedom
and liberation—to the Gospel in a way that considered, as
Dr. Copeland says, "the necessity and importance of the
Christian demand for holiness of life, for spiritual health.
It underscored the continuity between the essential freedom of human persons as such, and the effective or social
freedom that makes fully human living possible."[89] Dr.
Copeland, in a markedly different tone from Dr. Cone,

[87] Mt 6:14–15.
[88] *CCC* 1443.
[89] M. Shawn Copeland, "Method in Emerging Black Catholic Theology",
in *Taking Down Our Harps: Black Catholics in the United States*, ed. Cyprian
Davis, O.S.B., and Diana L. Hayes (Maryknoll, N.Y.: Orbis Books, 1998), 123.

says that black Catholic theology "carries within it the seed of universal concern that extends most particularly to all marginalized and oppressed persons and that advocate for the liberation of all—oppressed as well as the oppressor".[90]

Can black liberation theology, then, be utilized in a Catholic response to racism? I believe the answer is both yes and no. Yes, if the methodology used directs the faithful toward a deeper understanding and appreciation of the black experience, while acknowledging the dignity and value of all in the life of the Church. No, if the method used (1) points to an ecclesiology of oppressor and oppressed where people of color adopt a mindset of victimization, and (2) cultivates an approach to Christian anthropology, particularly in regard to the nature of sin and human freedom, that is not faithful to the objective truth of Church teaching.

Systematic theologian M. Shawn Copeland does an excellent job outlining the theological methods used in black Catholic theology that I believe can be useful in discussions of race. Among them, she lists "correlation" that "entails formulating questions from contemporary human experience, then showing how the Christian message of revelation provides adequate answers".[91] She also notes that black Catholic theologians want to hold their theological approach "accountable to the threefold interrelated criteria of orthodoxy, orthopathy, and orthopraxis". Dr. Copeland, utilizing the theological "foundations" approach of Bernard Lonergan, states that "theological foundations are grounded, not in religious propositions or the tradition or the culture or the social situation, but in the religiously, morally, intellectually converted persons." Lastly, she sees

[90] Ibid., 124.
[91] Ibid., 126.

"a commitment by theologians to seek truth, to embrace self-sacrifice and genuine humility, [and] to strive for holiness" [92] as playing key roles in the black Catholic theological method.

Dr. Copeland goes on to explain that black Catholic theology not only critiques social, political, economic, and cultural situations (like its liberation theology counterpart) but also critiques Catholic "traditions, symbols, and ecclesiastical structures" and utilizes a critical historical method of scriptural exegesis to uncover "stories of repression".[93] This approach is understandable given, as we have seen, that the Catholic Church in America failed to fully recognize the evil of slavery despite her own magisterial teaching and in light of her tragically weak response to Jim Crow segregation laws in the postbellum era.

These foundational principles of black Catholic theology are wedded to an authentic theology of liberation via the struggle for acceptance faced by black Catholics: the fundamental and pervasive struggle to be recognized, welcomed, and accepted as human persons.[94] As we saw earlier, black Catholic theology identifies four core elements that characterize black spirituality: contemplative (the intense awareness of always being in the presence of God), holistic (involves the whole person, body and soul), joyful (deeply passionate, vibrant, emotional), and communitarian ("I" finds meaning in "we").[95] Black spirituality affirms the

[92] Ibid., 127.

[93] Ibid., 128.

[94] See Bryan N. Massingale, S.T.D., *Racial Justice and the Catholic Church* (Maryknoll, N.Y.: Orbis Books, 2010), 19–21.

[95] See Joseph L. Howze et al., *"What We Have Seen and Heard": A Pastoral Letter on Evangelization from the Black Bishops of the United States* (Cincinnati: St. Anthony Messenger Press, 1984), 8–10, http://www.usccb.org/issues-and -action/cultural-diversity/african-american/resources/upload/what-we-have -seen-and-heard.pdf.

essential goodness and rightness of black existence, provides strength to face racism and prejudice, gives consolation in times of sorrow and rejection, and challenges black people to live ethically despite injustice and persecution.

The above black Catholic approach to theological method can be helpful in moving the dialogue on race forward to the extent that it sheds light on the historical experience of black Catholics, drawing nonblack believers into an empathetic response to those experiences. This opens the door to greater recognition, appreciation, and respect for the diverse gifts and talents of black Catholics in the life of the Church. This method should also hold the Church accountable to live faithfully what she believes and teaches in her doctrinal pronouncements.

Black Catholic theology is not helpful to the discussion of race, however, when yoked to a theology of liberation that does not ask what the Church is but, rather, what it means to be the Church within the limited context of liberating the poor and the oppressed. In this ecclesial vision, the Church's principal mission to evangelize the world in order to make Jesus known, loved, and served, which certainly includes challenging injustice and identifying herself with the poor, becomes muted by an unbalanced emphasis on liberating oppressed peoples. Fighting against injustice and working with the poor are important works of the Church that should be greatly emphasized, but this is not why the martyrs gave their lives or, when we fail to do these well, why young people leave the Church.

According to the worldview of the more radical branch of black liberation theology, *the "Church"* is, properly speaking, the oppressed People of God who have joined together seeking political means to remedy their subjugation while, in contrast, the *Church's Magisterium and hierarchy* are members of the oppressor class, since it does not participate in the class struggle. As one synopsis put it:

> The people demand more than hierarchy, more than structure, more than rules and regulations from the Catholic Church. African Americans especially have needs that go beyond the racist institutional structures of the United States Catholic Church. African American Catholics carry within us ... the rage of being despised and used by other human persons who deemed themselves superior to us. Our history unites us to Jesus, the Suffering Servant who dies alone and abandoned by his friends. We, too, have felt abandoned and alone in an alien country, and we still experience that abandonment and loneliness in the racist institutions of our society, perhaps particularly in the Church. It is a Church ... that prefers the safety of hierarchy to the radical, countercultural mission of Jesus to challenge the status quo and minister to the people; the people of God with all their beautiful diversity and individual needs, the little people who are the Church. It is our responsibility to begin rewriting the history of the Church so that as a community we glorify God ... not in materialistic, capitalistic expressions, but rather with a commitment to love, respect, forgive, and serve one another.[96]

Dr. Cone commented on this topic by stating that "black Catholics have little space for challenging the white Catholic Church.... The white ecclesiastical machinery with which black Catholics have to do battle is so powerful and determined in its own self-righteousness that blacks who dare challenge it had better be prepared for harsh and 'divinely' ordained punishment.... The white power structure in the Catholic Church is so restrictive

[96] Black Catholic Evangelization Forum, "Reclaiming and Rewriting Our Tradition", *Reach Out!*, November 1999, 1.

on what blacks can do or say that it is almost impossible to think creatively."[97]

This view of theology "from below" is shallow in its understanding of the hierarchical nature of the Church. It places the Magisterium on the same level as a secular corporation or governmental entity, comparing Church hierarchy and authority to the obdurate structure of a worldwide conglomerate. This impoverished ecclesiology ignores and disparages the fact that the Church is both "already" (temporal) and "not yet" (eschatological). She exists not merely as the Church on earth but also as the Church resplendent, as the glorified Body of Christ who established and sustains His Church as a *visible organization* through which He communicates grace and truth to all.[98] It is the *nature of the Church Herself*, founded and organized by Jesus Christ, that is holy despite *the sinfulness* of her members who, as I have previously stated, are in need of God's merciful love.

The *Catechism of the Catholic Church* explains, "The Church ... is held, as a matter of faith, to be unfailingly holy. This is because Christ, the Son of God, who with the Father and the Spirit is hailed as 'alone holy,' loved the Church as his Bride, giving himself up for her so as to sanctify her; he joined her to himself as his body and endowed her with the gift of the Holy Spirit for the glory of God."[99] It continues, "United with Christ, the Church is sanctified by him; through him and with him she becomes sanctifying. 'All the activities of the Church are directed, as toward their end, to the sanctification of men in Christ and the glorification of God' (*Sacrosanctum Concilium*,

---

[97] James H. Cone, *For My People: Black Theology and the Black Church* (Maryknoll, N.Y.: Orbis Books, 1996), 49, 51.

[98] Cf. Mt 16:16–18; 18:18; *Lumen Gentium*, nos. 1–17.

[99] *CCC* 823, quoting *Lumen Gentium*, no. 39. Cf. Eph 5:25–26.

no. 11). It is in the Church that 'the fullness of the means of salvation' (*Unitatis Redintegratio*, no. 3) has been deposited. It is in her that 'by the grace of God we acquire holiness' (*Lumen Gentium*, no. 48)."[100] The *Catechism* concludes, "'The Church on earth is endowed already with a sanctity that is real though imperfect' (*Lumen Gentium*, no. 48). In her members perfect holiness is something yet to be acquired."[101]

Thus, the Catholic Church, as the expert in humanity, "has the duty of proclaiming liberation in its deeper, fuller sense, the sense proclaimed and realized by Jesus," as Pope Saint John Paul II noted. "That fuller liberation is liberation from everything that oppresses human beings, but especially liberation from sin and the evil one."[102] To set us free from the bondage of sin and death, we need the indwelling love of Christ, which comes through the Holy Spirit, who leads us into all truth. It is the truth that sets us free,[103] and the truth of God's ever abundant and merciful love is rooted in freedom, a freedom *from* and a freedom *for*—the freedom *from* sin so that we can be free *for* God.

Black Catholic liberation theology also strongly identifies with the oppression of the Israelites by the Egyptians, and the subsequent freedom of God's Chosen People in the Exodus. Dr. Copeland notes that "the enslaved Africans placed their experience alongside that of the enslaved

---

[100] Ibid., 824. *Sacrosanctum Concilium* is Vatican II's Constitution on the Sacred Liturgy (December 4, 1963); *Unitatis Redintegratio* is Vatican II's Decree on Ecumenism (November 21, 1964).

[101] Ibid., 825.

[102] Pope John Paul II, Opening Address, 1978 Latin American Conference of Bishops (CELAM), Puebla, quoted in *The Pope and Revolution: John Paul II Confronts Liberation Theology*, ed. Quintin L. Quade (Washington, D.C.: Ethics and Public Policy Center, 1982), 66–67, https://www.ewtn.com/catholicism/library/retreat-of-liberation-theology-11017.

[103] Cf. Jn 8:31–38.

Hebrews.... God hears the cries and anguish of the people.... Egypt is a land of pain and suffering, of enslavement and oppression: the peoples' bondage is physical, political, economic, and spiritual."[104]

Care must be taken not to adopt a hermeneutical approach to Scripture that absolutizes the temporal aspects of freedom over the deeper spiritual meaning. As the Congregation for the Doctrine of the Faith notes in its document addressing liberation theology, there is no question that the Exodus event represents "freedom from foreign domination and from slavery", but it is also the "fundamental event in the formation of the chosen people" where "liberation is ordered to the foundation of the people of God and the Covenant cult celebrated on Mount Sinai. That is why the liberation of the Exodus cannot be reduced to a liberation which is principally or exclusively political in nature."[105] The politicization of the Gospel by liberation theology reduces its evangelizing witness and curtails its effectiveness when "the necessary struggle for human justice and freedom in the economic and political sense constitutes the whole essence of salvation."[106]

There are several black scholars who provide an interesting critique of black liberation theology. Anthony B. Bradley, Ph.D., drawing from the thinking of Columbia University professor Dr. John McWhorter, says that black liberation theology presents a flawed anthropology that fosters victimization. In other words, liberation theology

---

[104] M. Shawn Copeland, "Foundations for Catholic Theology in an African American Context", in *Black and Catholic: The Challenge and Gift of Black Folk—Contributions of African American Experience and Thought to Catholic Theology*, 2nd ed., ed. Jamie T. Phelps, O.P. (Milwaukee: Marquette University Press, 2002), 135.

[105] Congregation for the Doctrine of the Faith, Instruction on "Theology of Liberation", IV, 3.

[106] Ibid., VI, 4.

reduces the experience of black people to victims. Bradley states, "Victimology perpetuates a separatist and elitist platform that provides no opportunity for racial reconciliation. Victimology is an adoption of victimhood as the core of one's identity. It is a subconscious, culturally inherited affirmation that life for blacks in America has been in the past and will be in the future a life of being victimized by the oppression of whites."[107] He continues,

> Many blacks, infused with victimology, wield self-righteous indignation in the service of exposing the inadequacies of the "other" (e.g., white person) rather than finding a way forward. The perpetual belief in a racial identity born out of self-loathing and anxiety often leads to more time spent inventing reasons to cry racism then working towards changing social mores and often inhibits movement toward reconciliation and positive mobility.[108]

Victimization in black Catholic theology must be avoided at all cost. This can be done by focusing on the cardinal virtue of justice since the road to reconciliation is paved with justice and mercy. The *Catechism* reiterates that "justice toward men disposes one to respect the rights of each and to establish in human relationships the harmony that promotes equity with regard to persons and to the common good. The just man, often mentioned in the Sacred Scriptures, is distinguished by habitual right thinking and the uprightness of his conduct toward his neighbor."[109] The explication of the black Catholic experience through a careful exegesis of the historical and social narratives of the past, along with an honest assessment of the recurrent

---

[107] Anthony B. Bradley, *Liberating Black Theology: The Bible and the Black Experience in America* (Wheaton, Ill.: Crossway, 2010), 19.

[108] Ibid., 20.

[109] *CCC* 1807.

challenges facing race relations today, can lead to healing when authentic justice, rooted in the *imago Dei*, is recognized as a revelatory rather than a solely political, social, or economic outcome.

Victimization is allowing past events to control your present. We must acknowledge the reality of evil and must work hard to mitigate its effects by cultivating virtue—by helping to open the eyes of our brothers and sisters who are blinded by hatred and vitriol, and see the resplendent Light of Christ in every person. It is true that the past helps shape us into the person we are today, but the past does not determine our future. Our future (including where we will spend eternity) is determined by our decision made in freedom and love to accept or reject God's invitation to life-giving relationship with Him.

Black Catholic liberation theology must always remember that the primary liberation is from sin. Saint John Paul II, during his 1987 visit to the United States, called on black Catholics to "help us all to remember that *authentic freedom* comes from accepting the truth and from living one's life in accordance with it—and the full truth is found only in Christ Jesus." He challenged black Catholics to "inspire us by your desire to forgive—as Jesus forgave— and by your *desire to be reconciled* with all the people of this nation, even those who would unjustly deny you the full exercise of your human rights."[110]

When we use our freedom to conform ourselves to God's holy will—to be the person He created us to be by living in a way commensurate with this truth—then we are spiritually free. We realize spiritual freedom when

[110] Pope John Paul II, Meeting with the Black Catholic Community of New Orleans (September 12, 1987), no. 3 (emphasis in original), https://www .vatican.va/content/john-paul-ii/en/speeches/1987/september/documents/hf _jp-ii_spe_19870912_cattolici-new-orleans.html.

we lovingly accept God's grace in accord with who we are called to be. When we are spiritually free, we are liberated from our fallen condition and directed toward union with God. At the center of God's plan for human freedom is the fact that He created man in the Light of Christ so that we can participate in God's own Trinitarian life. This is humanity's truest identity. As Pope John Paul II states beautifully in *Veritatis Splendor*,

> This effort by the Church finds its support—the "secret" of its educative power— not so much in doctrinal statements and pastoral appeals to vigilance, as in *constantly looking to the Lord Jesus*. Each day the Church looks to Christ with unfailing love, fully aware that the true and final answer to the problem of morality lies in him alone. In a particular way, it is *in the Crucified Christ* that *the Church finds the answer* to the question troubling so many people today: how can obedience to universal and unchanging moral norms respect the uniqueness and individuality of the person, and not represent a threat to his freedom and dignity? ... *The Crucified Christ reveals the authentic meaning of freedom; he lives it fully in the total gift of himself* and calls his disciples to share in his freedom.[111]

Gerhard Ludwig Cardinal Müller, the former prefect of the Vatican's Congregation for the Doctrine of the Faith, succinctly summarizes the relationship between human dignity and the object of true liberation when he said, "Man lives in this world, in a world created by God, but he also has a divine and eternal universal vocation. The Church's task today is coexisting in modern society, but at the same time underscoring that man's ultimate aim is the Triune God, the God made man, the God of love. If we

---

[111] *Veritatis Splendor*, no. 85; emphasis in original.

forget the ultimate aim, we cannot argue anything in favor of human dignity, because we can speak of equality among men only if we refer to God."[112]

In the fight against racial injustice, black Catholic theology can help people of good will see that humanity is created yearning for fullness while still mired in concupiscence. Due to our fallen nature, we become frustrated when faced with the reality of human frailty and weakness—when confronted with the fact that we cannot on our own love as God loves. Spiritual freedom comes when we love with the love of Christ, but sin impedes our efforts to make this choice. It is in this way that sin is enslaving: it binds us to disordered love. The more sin becomes a habit, the more it binds us to the fleeting goods of this world—our disordered attachments. Sin establishes an addictive pattern and keeps us from conforming to the truth of our being.

It is our free choice that needs to be liberated, and it is Christ who accomplishes this through his death and Resurrection. We need God's love dwelling within us to free us from the bondage of sin so we can become witnesses of that love to the world.

Understandably, there is a sense of impatience when it comes to the sin of racism. "We've been dealing with this issue for hundreds of years, Lord. How much longer?" The fight to end racism is long and arduous, and it cannot be undertaken without courage, stamina, and fortitude. The close affinity between the Israelites and blacks—two God-fearing peoples who share historical instances of chattel slavery—gave birth to a number of Negro spirituals that

[112] Quoted in Andrea Gagliarducci, "Cardinal: Liberation Theology Needed Separation from Marxism", Catholic News Agency, February 25, 2014, https://www.catholicnewsagency.com/news/29110/cardinal-liberation-theology-needed-separation-from-marxism.

echo the experience of oppressed people. Many of these hymns are sung in black Catholic churches throughout the United States to this day and serve as a hauntingly beautiful reminder of God's grace and mercy toward His people.

Inspired by the sung praises of Israel and the Negro spiritual traditions, let us trust in God that He will bring to an end all that divides us and reflect on Psalm 13:

> [*For the Choirmaster. A Psalm of David.*]
> How long, O Lord, will you forget me?
>   How long will you hide your face?
> How long must I bear grief in my soul,
>   this sorrow in my heart day and night?
>   How long shall my enemy prevail?
>
> Look at me, answer me, Lord my God!
>   Give light to my eyes lest I fall asleep in death,
> lest my enemy say: "I have overcome him";
>   lest my foes rejoice to see my fall.
>
> As for me, I trust in your merciful love.
>   Let my heart rejoice in your saving help:
> Let me sing to the Lord for his goodness to me,
>   singing psalms to the name of the Lord, the Most
>   High.[113]

---

[113] Ps 13:1–6, in *The Abbey Psalter: The Book of Psalms Used by the Trappist Monks of Genesee Abbey* by Abbot John Eudes Bamberger (Mahwah, N.J.: Paulist Press), 1981.

CHAPTER FIVE

The Black Lives Matter Movement

In July 2020, I was scheduled to appear as a guest on the Australian Catholic radio show *The Catholic Toolbox* with host George Manassa. A week before the broadcast, George posted a social media advertisement on Instagram and Facebook announcing that we would be discussing the Black Lives Matter movement.

Almost instantly I began losing followers and started receiving snarky remarks and angry comments like "I'm shocked, Deacon. How can you support them?" Simply stating the words "black lives matter" spurred a vitriolic reaction that surprised me since there were no details of exactly what perspective George and I would be taking.

A few days after the post, George asked me if he should take it down. I told him, "No. Now people will actually listen to what I have to say."

In and of themselves there is absolutely nothing wrong with the words "black lives matter" as a declared social construct or a statement of truth. Black lives do indeed matter.

I would even say the words "black lives matter" should not be diluted by stating another noble truth: "all lives matter". Of course, they do. It needs to be understood that declaring that "black lives matter" is not to say that other lives do not matter or that they are of less importance. The statement does not negate the dignity of all human persons nor assumes that all white people are racists simply because they are white—nor alienates anyone by placing people of color above other races.

The words, at their heart, speak to the angst and frustration of black people who have endured centuries of exploitation, abuse, mistrust, suspicion, humiliation (the list goes on). To replace "black lives matter" with "all lives matter" feels to many people like others may be indifferent and unsympathetic to our pain. The words express a desire to raise awareness and draw attention to our plight—to shine a light in the darkness.

Sometimes words are not enough and must be translated into action. Organizing peaceful marches and rallies to protest the inequitable treatment of people of color by those in authority, like the indomitable Reverend Dr. Martin Luther King, Jr., did in his day, is laudable, and Catholics of good conscience should feel free to participate in such events.

The reason there is tremendous controversy and, quite frankly, outright rage over the words "black lives matter" is that they have become conflated with, and almost exclusively identified with, the Black Lives Matter (BLM) movement. BLM has been associated with utter hatred toward white people, as well as being the machine behind violence-ridden protests that spurred vandalism, rioting, and looting in many major cities across the United States.

Is there any truth to these accusations, or are they simply spurious background noise designed to divert attention away from dealing with the issue of race? Can BLM serve as a legitimate Catholic response to racism?

BLM started as a social media post expressing outrage over the George Zimmerman acquittal in the shooting death of Trayvon Martin in 2013. The post was reshared with the #BlackLivesMatter hashtag and a movement was born.

The original focus of BLM was not only to raise awareness of racism but to inspire the next generation of activists.

The movement grew quickly as incidents between police officers and people of color became more widely reported. Marches and protests were organized, and the BLM social media following grew exponentially with millions of followers by 2018. As BLM gained prominence, their objectives and goals began to shift, encompassing a wider spectrum of issues beyond race. Olga M. Segura describes this evolution in *Birth of a Movement: Black Lives Matter and the Catholic Church*:

> One of the goals of Black Lives Matter ... is to fight for a world free of all of the systems that oppress and kill Black people—including policing and prisons. The movement ... promotes an unrelenting commitment to human life and dignity. [BLM] activists ... center the lived experiences of society's most vulnerable, Black transgender and queer women and men.... [The BLM founders] are committed to ensuring that BLM helps to dismantle the systemic oppression caused by cisgender white women and men.... If our church leaders were not ready to dismantle our institution's white supremacy, then young Catholics ... must use the intersectional, anticapitalist, and Catholic framework of Black Lives Matter to demand a better church.[1]

The philosophical and theological underpinnings of BLM should sound familiar since it is drawn directly from critical race theory and Marxist-influenced liberation theology. Segura continues,

> Liberation theology calls on Catholics to study Jesus' teachings through the experiences of the world's most

---

[1] Olga M. Segura, *Birth of a Movement: Black Lives Matter and the Catholic Church* (Maryknoll, N.Y.: Orbis Books, 2021), 11–13.

marginalized people, using the economic theories of Friedrich Engels and Karl Marx. Like liberation theology, Black Lives Matter prioritizes the experiences of the poorest and most oppressed.[2]

BLM states that it "is not a movement pushing an extremist agenda that contradicts [the Catholic] faith; it is a secular version of our Catholic social teaching."[3] Yet, the 2020 "About" section of the Black Lives Matter website paints a very different picture, which has since been revised to soften the language and has removed many of the statements quoted below:

We are guided by the fact that all Black lives matter, regardless of actual or perceived sexual identity, gender identity, gender expression, economic status, ability, disability, religious beliefs or disbeliefs, immigration status, or location.

We make space for transgender brothers and sisters to participate and lead.

We are self-reflexive and do the work required to dismantle cisgender privilege and uplift Black trans folk, especially Black trans women who continue to be disproportionately impacted by trans-antagonistic violence.

We build a space that affirms Black women and is free from sexism, misogyny, and environments in which men are centered.

We disrupt the Western-prescribed nuclear family structure requirement by supporting each other as extended families and "villages" that collectively care for one another, especially our children, to the degree that mothers, parents, and children are comfortable.

[2] Ibid., 16.
[3] Ibid., 19.

We foster a queeraffirming network. When we gather, we do so with the intention of freeing ourselves from the tight grip of heteronormative thinking, or rather, the belief that all in the world are heterosexual.[4]

Clearly, BLM is using prejudice and racial injustice as a Trojan horse to advance their true agenda: the promotion and normalization of alternative lifestyle choices as well as the destruction of the nuclear family consisting of one man (fathers) and one woman (mothers). Using the ideologies of critical race theory and liberation theology rooted in Marxism, BLM, following Dr. James Cone's ideology, expands the definition of "oppressed" and "marginalized" beyond race to include homosexual and transgendered individuals, while openly criticizing the Catholic Church for defending the traditional family and not following the BLM lead.

I would like to look at three aspects of BLM in more detail as a litmus test to discover if they truly advocate healing racial divisions: (1) the claim that BLM "is not a movement pushing an extremist agenda that contradicts" Catholicism, (2) the statement that BLM "promotes an unrelenting commitment to human life and dignity", and (3) that BLM is "a secular version of our Catholic social teaching".

Claim No. 1: BLM Does Not Contradict Catholicism

A more accurate statement regarding if BLM contradicts Catholicism would be that BLM "is not a movement pushing an extremist agenda that contradicts *our version* of Catholicism". Actively encouraging, supporting, and promoting the same-sex and transgender lifestyles and

[4] Black Lives Matter website, "About" page, accessed May 14, 2020, https://blacklivesmatter.com/about/.

disrupting "the Western-prescribed nuclear family structure" are blatant contradictions of the Catholic faith.

The Catholic Church upholds the dignity of every human person regardless of race, class, gender, or religious affiliation because we are all created in God's image and likeness. The Catholic principle is simple: we love everyone but we do not always love a person's actions, and we judge actions; we never judge people. God alone is the judge. As James says in his Letter, "There is one lawgiver and judge, he who is able to save and to destroy."[5]

BLM, in lockstep with a morally relativistic society, fails to make the distinction between the human person and his actions and behaviors. According to this way of thinking, responding to my sensual appetites is an expression of my person, and my sexual preferences define my identity. In addressing this issue, the Congregation for Catholic Education stated that

> [Gender] ideology inspires educational programmes and legislative trends that promote ideas of personal identity and affective intimacy that make a radical break with the actual *biological difference* between male and female. Human identity is consigned to the individual's choice, which can also change in time. These ideas are the expression of a widespread way of thinking and acting in today's culture that confuses "genuine freedom with the idea that each individual can act arbitrarily as if there were no truths, values and principles to provide guidance, and everything were possible and permissible" (*Amoris Laetitia*, no. 34).[6]

---

[5] Jas 4:12.

[6] Congregation for Catholic Education, *"Male and Female He Created Them": Towards a Path of Dialogue on the Question of Gender Theory in Education* (February 2, 2019), no. 22 (emphasis in original), https://www.vatican.va/roman_curia/congregations/ccatheduc/documents/rc_con_ccatheduc_doc_20190202_maschio-e-femmina_en.pdf. *Amoris Laetitia* (The Joy of Love) is a post-synodal apostolic exhortation by Pope Francis (March 19, 2016).

God is the author of nature and thus the author of natural law; to live in accord with natural law is to live in accord with God's will. The condition of Original Sin or fallen nature brought with it disordered passions and desires. After the Fall, humans began to act against their nature. As a result, all human persons are imperfect—that is, in an "unnatural" and "disordered" condition.

Human passions and reason are both appetites and, as such, act as guides to moral behavior. Simply stated, human activity and actions originating from these natural appetites that are directed toward virtue are good (ordered actions), while activities and actions directed toward vice are evil (disordered actions). Again, we are talking about actions and decisions, not persons.

The *Catechism of the Catholic Church* teaches that homosexual sexual activity and transgenderism are considered incompatible with the natural law and God's plan for human sexuality:

Homosexuality refers to relations between men or between women who experience an exclusive or predominant sexual attraction toward persons of the same sex. It has taken a great variety of forms through the centuries and in different cultures. Its psychological genesis remains largely unexplained. Basing itself on Sacred Scripture, which presents homosexual acts as acts of grave depravity (cf. Gen 19:1–29; Rom 1:24–27; 1 Cor 6:10; 1 Tim 1:10), tradition has always declared that "homosexual acts are intrinsically disordered" (Congregation for the Doctrine of the Faith, *Persona Humana*, no. 8). They are contrary to the natural law. They close the sexual act to the gift of life. They do not proceed from a genuine affective and sexual complementarity. Under no circumstances can they be approved.[7]

---

[7] CCC 2357.

I can imagine some people, even Catholics, reading words like "grave depravity" and "intrinsically disordered" may get upset and say to themselves, "This is a hard teaching. Who can accept it?" Some Catholic advocates of homosexual behavior—in an attempt to reassess and alter Church teaching to fit their subjective, secular ideology—have suggested a change in the language of the *Catechism* from "intrinsically disordered" to "differently ordered". This is absolutely unacceptable. Whatever is said to be "natural" or "ordered" is in accord with what is objectively true, good, and beautiful for human persons. What is called "unnatural" or "disordered" is discordant with that which is objectively true, good, and beautiful for humanity. The BLM and relativistic Catholics are using the hands of moral relativism to manipulate the modeling clay of objective moral truth in an attempt to reshape it into disordered and subjective so-called "truth" that fits the cultural narrative of "tolerance" and "diversity", which labels people who do not agree with them as "haters", "transphobic", and "close-minded". What does any of this have to do with black lives mattering and healing the sin of racism?

Catholics can, however, stand in solidarity with those who have experienced discrimination, prejudice, and even violence because of their homosexual and transgendered orientation. At all times we must recognize the full human dignity of every person. Not to do so would be a blatant contradiction of the virtues of justice and charity. Indeed, considerable love and acceptance should be extended to our homosexual and transgendered brothers and sisters who often find themselves in a state of anxiety, loneliness, and rejection.

It cannot be stated enough that we are called to see the image and likeness of God in every person, especially in our enemies and those who disagree with us. Make no mistake: with the love of Christ, the Catholic Church loves our transgendered brothers and sisters and those with same-sex attraction. We love them enough not to lie to them. Grounded in natural law principles together with Sacred Scripture and Sacred Tradition, the Church has taught that the proper use of the sexual faculty is between a male and female who are in a state of matrimony and who are open to having children. The conjugal act is meant to be an expression of loving and life-giving union by virtue of a husband and wife's matrimonial commitment. Sexual intercourse between members of the same sex is understood to be an incongruous use of the gift of sexuality. The act itself does not serve to create a loving and potentially life-giving bond between male and female, and therefore by its very nature, the act itself cannot be open to the possibility of bringing forth new life. Nor is it properly "person-uniting", where in sexual intercourse between a man and a woman the two form a person-uniting oneness that by its nature expresses a person-creating love. Even in cases where, due to circumstance, age, or health condition, procreation cannot occur, the sexual union of a man and a woman remains the *kind* of union by which new human beings come to be.

It is very important to note that whether persons are same-sex attracted or transgendered, the Church does not see them as less valuable. They have the same sacred dignity as everyone else. They, too, are children of God and brothers and sisters in Christ. Although the Church teaches that the homosexual and transgendered conditions involve disordered inclinations and misperceptions of human sexuality, it does not teach that the persons themselves are necessarily sinful or less valuable as human persons. So while individuals may have little or no responsibility for having a confused orientation, they can exercise moral agency in respect to their decisions and actions.

Consequently, our transgendered brothers and sisters and those with same-sex attraction are called to fulfil their need for intimacy not only through a deep and loving relationship with Jesus Christ, but also through rich human relationships and close friendships, by extending and sharing their love more broadly to the wider community and, in some cases, to matrimony, that is, between a Christian man and woman (sacramental), or a Christian man and non-Christian woman (nonsacramental) or vice versa. This expectation is not unrealistic and cruel. As Jesus teaches in Matthew's Gospel, "If any man would come after me, let him deny himself and take up his cross and follow me. For whoever would save his life will lose it, and whoever loses his life for my sake will find it."[8] It is the Gospel lived out in a love that surpasses all understanding.

According to their 2020 "About" web page, cited above, the BLM movement also wants to help "dismantle" the systemic oppression caused by "cisgender privilege" (i.e., white women and men) and "disrupt the Western-prescribed nuclear family structure requirement". The first statement, which blames white people alone for problems in black communities, is not only infused with Dr. James Cone's ideology, but is also straight out of the Marxist playbook that imbues a victimization mentality. As Dr. Anthony B. Bradley notes,

> Marx often uses broad generalizations, many times unsubstantiated, to establish the identity of those he defines as victims. This pattern ... produces broad generalizations that often take the form of describing the whole of the black experience in America as one of being victimized by white oppression.[9]

The ironic thing is that BLM misinterprets Marxism in its application of personal status. For example, Karl Marx

[8] Mt 16:24–25.
[9] Anthony B. Bradley, *Liberating Black Theology: The Bible and the Black Experience in America* (Wheaton, Ill.: Crossway, 2010), 102.

applied the term "oppressed" in relation to blue-collar workers in manually repetitive jobs where the nature of the work reduces the worker to a cog in the machine, thereby depersonalizing him. BLM and others, borrowing from Marx, use the term "oppressed" as a juxtaposition to describe the situation of blacks at the hands of whites. However, as Dr. Bradley points out, Marx used "oppression" within a historical justification framework that stated

> justice is discerned according to the demand of a certain historical context—the autonomous experience of a collection of individuals. In one context, according to Marx, certain practices may be permissible, while in another they would be unethical. For example, certain forms of slavery and oppression were considered to be justified at various stages in history ... [and that] slavery, once it became economically questionable, could be justifiably abolished.[10]

By adopting Marxian ideology uncritically, the BLM movement has undermined its own credibility and rhetoric, driving the wedge further between the races rather than working to bring people together.

Regarding the family, BLM sees men and fathers as the antagonistic oppressors of women; therefore, they want to reenvision families "free from sexism, misogyny, and environments in which men are centered", according to their 2020 "About" web page. Clearly, these are the musings of radical feminists who hate men.

In one sense, I can understand their frustration. Men are the predominate consumers of pornography, the primary

---

[10] Ibid. For a more in-depth discussion of this aspect of Karl Marx's thought, see Thomas Sowell, *Marxism: Philosophy and Economics* (New York: Quill, 1985), and R. G. Peffer, *Marxism, Morality, and Social Justice* (Princeton, N.J.: Princeton University Press, 1990).

benefactors of human sex trafficking (modern-day slavery), the main perpetrators of rape, and possess a culturally encouraged hit-it-and-quit-it mentality, all of which objectify women, reducing them to mere objects of pleasure and gratification. As a man, I am greatly angered and troubled by this behavior as well, but the blame cannot be placed solely on the shoulders of white people. It will be helpful to take a historical look back to see how we got to where we are today.

From the 1600s, when the first black people in America were enslaved by white people, until the mid-1900s, black parents strove to open doors for their children and to create opportunities for them to succeed, as best they could, despite the seemingly insurmountable barriers of racial oppression and poverty. Black families, led by fathers and mothers, strove to lift a veil of ignorance from a society that held them down, condemned them to slavery, and denied them educational opportunities, thus limiting them to working as unskilled, cheap laborers. Segregation, redlining, and other unjust practices exacerbated the problem. Yet, in the face of tremendous adversity, black nuclear families remained *together*, as late as 1960, the percentage of black families that were headed by husbands and wives was 61 percent.[11]

This number steadily declined during the latter half of the twentieth century, and today almost 54 percent of children of color are born to single mothers who are far more likely than married mothers to be undereducated and poor.[12] As marriage and family life declined within the

[11] Dawne Mouzon, "Why Has Marriage Declined Among Black Americans?", Scholars Strategy Network, accessed April 27, 2023, https://scholars.org/brief/why-has-marriage-declined-among-black-americans.

[12] "The American Family Today", Pew Research Center, accessed April 27, 2023, https://www.pewresearch.org/social-trends/2015/12/17/1-the-american-family-today/.

black community, many men of color have embraced an increasingly hedonistic culture, turning their backs on the responsibility of fatherhood and commitment to lifelong relationships. So, as Kay S. Hymowitz notes, "the truth is that we are now a two-family nation, separate and unequal—one thriving and intact, and the other struggling, broken, and far too often"[13] people of color. She continues:

> Policy elites [have tried] to frame what was really the broad cultural problem of separate and unequal families as a simple lack-of-reproductive-services problem. Ergo, girls "at risk" must need sex education and contraceptive services....
>
> They did not follow the middle-class life script that read: protracted adolescence, college, first job, marriage—and only then children. They did not share the belief that children needed mature, educated mothers who would make their youngsters' development the center of their lives. Access to birth control couldn't change any of that....
>
> Teen pregnancy not only failed to go down, despite all the public attention, the tens of millions of dollars, and the birth control pills that were thrown its way. *It went up*—peaking in 1990 at 117 pregnancies per 1,000 teenage girls.... About 80 percent of those young girls who became mothers were single, and the vast majority would be poor.[14]

Today, the situation has not improved. More than 50 percent of black children are still born to unmarried

---

[13] Kay S. Hymowitz, "The Black Family: 40 Years of Lies", *City Journal*, Summer 2005, https://www.city-journal.org/html/black-family-40-years-lies -12872.html.

[14] Ibid.; emphasis in original.

mothers.[15] Hip-hop culture glamorizes thug life. The acceptance and legalization of so-called gay "marriage" has led to the idea that children growing up with their own married parents consisting of a mother and father is a form of discrimination. In some states, like Washington and California, children suffering from gender dysphoria can begin hormone therapy regimens and undergo "gender reassignment" surgeries without parental consent. Organizations like BLM see families headed by fathers as a potential source of female oppression. These already tragic situations should not be worsened by dismantling nuclear families. Rather, we should endeavor to strengthen and revitalize the domestic church. In its document on the dignity of the human person, the Congregation for the Doctrine of the Faith states that

> respect for that dignity is owed to every human being because each one carries in an indelible way his own dignity and value. *The origin of human life has its authentic context in marriage and in the family*, where it is generated through an act which expresses the reciprocal love between a man and a woman. Procreation which is truly responsible vis-à-vis the child to be born "must be the fruit of marriage" (Congregation for the Doctrine of the Faith, instruction *Donum Vitae*, II, A, 1).... "Natural law, which is at the root of the recognition of true equality between persons and peoples, deserves to be recognized as the source that inspires the relationship between the spouses in their responsibility for begetting new children.

[15] For all racial and ethnic groups combined, 38.6 percent of births in the United States were out of wedlock. For blacks, the number is 54.9 percent; American Indians or Alaska Natives, 54.4 percent; Native Hawaiians or other Pacific Islanders, 58.9 percent; Hispanics, 55.8 percent; whites, 27.6 percent; and Asians, 13.7 percent. Michelle J.K. Osterman et al., "Births: Final Data for 2020", *National Vital Statistics Reports* 70, no. 17 (February 7, 2022), Table 11, p. 28, https://www.cdc.gov/nchs/data/nvsr70/nvsr70-17.pdf.

The transmission of life is inscribed in nature and its laws stand as an unwritten norm to which all must refer" (Pope Benedict XVI, Address to the Participants in the International Congress, May 10, 2008).[16]

The process of rebuilding families from a Catholic perspective starts with making loving and life-giving communion with God the heart and center of family life. In communities of color specifically, the emphasis should not be on pointing fingers at white people to accuse and blame. We must look inward and begin answering some serious questions of our own.

Are we so preoccupied and distracted with worldly ideology that we fail to notice what is happening to our children, who, in the midst of a cultural onslaught, opt for no religious affiliation at all? Why have street gangs and drug cartels replaced families? Why do we tolerate black-on-black violence? Why do men refer to women as bitches and whores? Why do we tolerate an entire generation of fathers who have physically, emotionally, or spiritually abandoned their wives and children? When will black Americans stop murdering half a million of our own children every year through abortion? How can people of color rediscover the beauty and truth of our heritage, and renew the commitment to live our spirituality with boldness, fidelity, and enthusiasm? Where are our husbands and fathers to help lead and guide the next generation?

Unraveling the tangled web of racism, while extremely important work, cannot be the sole response to the institutional dehumanization that marks our modern culture, since solving racism *alone* cannot answer the deeper, more serious

---

[16] Congregation for the Doctrine of the Faith, Instruction on Certain Bioethical Questions *Dignitas Personae* (September 8, 2008), no. 6 (emphasis in original), https://www.vatican.va/roman_curia/congregations/cfaith/documents/rc_con_cfaith_doc_20081208_dignitas-personae_en.html.

questions that need to be explored regarding the renewal of family life. This would be an incredibly enriching and rewarding task for the BLM movement to undertake. This is how we work together to make black lives matter.

Claim No. 2: BLM Promotes an Unrelenting Commitment to Human Life and Dignity

The secular framework that needs to be dismantled can be summed up in one phrase, popularized by Pope Saint John Paul II: the culture of death. This is a serious challenge for the entire Body of Christ, but it has particular import for communities of color today. Catholic teaching on the dignity of every person is consistent and clear. The Congregation for the Doctrine of the Faith notes that "the respect for the individual human being, which reason requires, is further enhanced and strengthened in the light of [the] truths of faith: thus, we see that there is no contradiction between the affirmation of the dignity and the affirmation of the sacredness of human life."[17]

BLM contradicts their own statement of belief in the "unrelenting commitment to human life" since they believe black women should exercise their "'fundamental right' to make their own reproductive choices. They believe that defending the 'right' of women who wish to end their pregnancy is greater than the 'supposed right to life' of the fetus,"[18] writes Bishop Edward K. Braxton.

Regarding the life issue, Bishop Braxton notes that "Black women continue to have the highest abortion rate of any racial or ethnic group.... For every 1,000 live births,

---

[17] Ibid., no. 7.

[18] Bishop Edward K. Braxton, "The Catholic Church and the Black Lives Matter Movement", in *The Church and the Racial Divide: Reflections of an African American Catholic Bishop* (Maryknoll, N.Y.: Orbis Books, 2021), 57.

there were 483 abortions. Although African Americans represent only 13 percent of the population of this country, between 2007 and 2010, almost 36 percent of the abortion deaths in the nation were Black infants."[19] A Center for Disease Control survey of 30 states in 2020 revealed that non-Hispanic Black women accounted for 39.2% of all abortions, the highest percentage of any group.[20] Catholic speaker Gloria Purvis adds that, in the black community, "abortion is shrinking our churches, schools, communities and congressional districts, as well as our future."[21]

According to the powerful documentary *MAAFA 21*, "Since 1993, legal abortion has killed more African Americans than AIDS, cancer, diabetes, heart disease, and violent crime combined. Every week, more blacks die in American abortion clinics than were killed in the entire Vietnam War."[22] The purveyors of the culture of death want us to embrace their eugenic ideology as status quo. They would like us to ignore the fact that abortion "kills as many African American people every four days as the Ku Klux Klan killed in 150 years".[23] The traffickers of subjective truth want to convince us that abortion and euthanasia are merely political or civil rights issues. In reality, marketing slogans such as "low-income health care", "reproductive rights", and "family planning" are simply euphemisms used by those who are trying to exterminate unborn and defenseless human persons as if they were vermin.

[19] Ibid.

[20] "Abortion Surveillance—United States, 2020", Center for Disease Control and Prevention, accessed April 27, 2023, https://www.cdc.gov/mmwr/volumes/71/ss/ss7110a1.htm#T6_down.

[21] Gloria Purvis, "What Will It Take to Respect Life in the Black Community?" (lecture, National Black Catholic Convocation I, Indianapolis, Ind., April 21, 2004).

[22] Excerpt from *MAAFA 21: Black Genocide in the 21st Century* (Denton, Tex.: Life Dynamics, 2009), DVD.

[23] Excerpt from ibid.

As a community of believers in Jesus Christ, Catholics of color do a great job of raising awareness about important issues such as poverty, racism, and civil rights, but if we continue to kill ourselves through this egregious abuse of our freedom, there will not be enough of us around for anyone to notice. When we allow abortion, we actually assist in and encourage the elimination of our brothers and sisters, something that hate groups could not accomplish for decades in this country. For true followers of Christ, and indeed for all people of goodwill, abortion is not about opinion or choice: it is a matter of life and death.

If BLM truly values human life and dignity, then why not speak for the voiceless—the innocent, most vulnerable victims of oppression in the womb? This is how we work together to make black lives matter.

Claim No. 3: BLM Is a Secular Version of Our Catholic Social Teaching

The basic principles of Catholic social teaching, as listed by the United States Conference of Catholic Bishops' Department of Justice, Peace, and Human Development, include the life and dignity of the human person; the call to family, community, and participation; rights and responsibilities; option for the poor and vulnerable; the dignity of work and the rights of workers; solidarity; and care for God's creation.[24]

Given the focus of BLM, and the fact that the life and dignity of the human person and family life have already

---

[24] A detailed explanation of each Catholic social justice principle can be found on the USCCB's website at https://www.usccb.org/beliefs-and-teachings/what-we-believe/catholic-social-teaching/seven-themes-of-catholic-social-teaching.

been explored, and the specific emphasis of this book on race, I will examine BLM and the Catholic social principle of solidarity. Specifically, I will consider the relationship between BLM and solidarity regarding violence, the Church, and the Gospel.

Ever since the Black Lives Matter movement gained prominence, I have been an outspoken critic of what they stand for, to the point of not seeing any purpose of engaging in dialogue with them and openly declaring that Catholics should have nothing to do with BLM.[25] However, after reading numerous essays by Bishop Edward K. Braxton, I now believe that Catholics should be open to establishing a dialogue with BLM, as difficult as those conversations may be. Although Catholics cannot support BLM at this juncture (for the reasons I am outlining in this chapter), there is no harm in having open and honest dialogue with those we disagree with. We should commit ourselves, as Bishop Braxton says, "to praying, listening, learning, thinking, and acting in ways that will help ... bridge the racial divide".[26]

Bishop Braxton outlines the historical reasons why focusing on solidarity—coming together as the Body of Christ—is vitally important to the discussion of race.

A past marred by racial oppression and systematic discrimination cannot be undone by pastoral letters, no matter how heartfelt they may be. The evil of America's original sin of enslaving free human beings ... has left a permanent scar on the nation's psyche. As a result, "white" Christianity lacks credibility to many members of the traditional

---

[25] See, for example, my comments in "Catholic Reporter's Notebook: Black Lives Matter", by Brian Fraga, *On the Catholic Beat* (blog), July 21, 2020, https://deaconharold.com/wp-content/uploads/2020/07/Catholic-Reporter%E2%80%99s-Notebook_-Black-Lives-Matter-_-Brian-Fraga.pdf.

[26] Braxton, "Catholic Church and Black Lives Matter Movement", 62.

> Black Church.... Historically, the Catholic Church has not been actively engaged in conversation with African American communities at the level of ideas, major movements, and the emergence of black consciousness.... While there is a degree of awareness of the Church's various social, educational, and healthcare ministries that make a positive contribution to black communities, the primary impression some movement supporters have of the church is that it is a large, white, conservative institution that stands aloof from confrontational movements such as Black Lives Matter.[27]

Utilizing the Catholic social principle of solidarity is a means of finding common ground so that there can be a starting point for meaningful discussion devoid of polemics and violent confrontation. The United States Conference of Catholic Bishops teach that

> we are one human family whatever our national, racial, ethnic, economic, and ideological differences. We are our brothers' and sisters' keepers, wherever they may be. Loving our neighbor has global dimensions in a shrinking world. At the core of the virtue of solidarity is the pursuit of justice and peace. Pope Paul VI taught that "if you want peace, work for justice." The Gospel calls us to be peacemakers. Our love for all our sisters and brothers demands that we promote peace in a world surrounded by violence and conflict.[28]

After the homicide of Mr. George Floyd, households were inundated with news reports night after night showing protesters taking to the streets marching with signs, holding rallies, and giving speeches. Some protesters wore

---

[27] Ibid., 46–47, 49.

[28] United States Conference of Catholic Bishops, "Solidarity", USCCB .org, accessed January 4, 2023, https://www.usccb.org/beliefs-and-teachings /what-we-believe/catholic-social-teaching/solidarity.

masks and engaged in rioting, looting, vandalism, and other blatant acts of violence while shouting, "Black lives matter!" Many who saw this began to associate these cowardly acts with BLM. Bishop Braxton observes that "leaders within the movement, however, stress that they reject violence and say those who speak of harming police are speaking in their own names and not in the name of the movement."[29]

If this is the case, BLM should be more outspoken in condemning violence committed in their name. They should be in solidarity with business owners, some of whom spent their life savings choosing to do business in neighborhoods that serve and employ people of color. The BLM movement highlights the fact that people of color have been victims of violence for years, so it only makes sense that they should be in solidarity with those who are victims of violence today, including the unborn. BLM has a tremendous opportunity to take the lead in bringing people together, to be catalyst for real change. Sadly, BLM chooses instead, Bishop Braxton says, to "embrace a radical theology of inclusion inspired by a revolutionary Jesus. They prefer a Jesus who spent more time confronting the power structure of Judaism and the Roman Empire than a Jesus who was turning the other cheek."[30]

Regarding the Church, theologian Jamie T. Phelps, O.P., lays a strong foundation upon which solidarity in communion can be built.

> First, the church creates the *community of believers* who grow in union with the triune God through their participation in the sacraments and the life of the church. Second, the church is called to be *a transformative agent in a divided community of believers* both Christian and non-Christian. And third, the church is called to be a *transformative agent in a*

---

[29] Braxton, "Catholic Church and Black Lives Matter Movement", 44.
[30] Ibid., 51.

world divided by sin and injustice.... Jesus's mission, which the church is called to continue, is primarily a mission of enabling all human beings to live in the fullness of their humanity as free and responsible human creatures made in the image of likeness of God. Such a life is only possible in the context of a radical communion, a union with God, with all human beings, and with the universe. Such a radical communion is born of deep contemplative prayer and God's gracious self-gift. God's grace alone enables us to live in right relationships with one another and all creation.[31]

Solidarity in communion (*koinonia*) emerged as one the most significant and preeminent images and insights in the post-conciliar period; it is the central reality of the Church and a major conduit for bridging the racial chasm.

The Church, because of its sacramental nature, establishes and brings us into *koinonia* with God and, consequently, into communion with all of humanity. The *relational* dynamic of God was the foundational truth revealed in the Second Vatican Council's *Dei Verbum*: that God reveals himself for the purpose of establishing relationship and, in doing so, reveals His own relational nature: Father, Son, and Holy Spirit. The *Catechism of the Catholic Church* reiterates that "the highest exemplar and source of this mystery is the unity, in the Trinity of Persons."[32] It is the relational nature of God, revealed to us most fully in Jesus Christ, who reveals our own nature to ourselves and, the *Catechism* continues, "restore[s] the unity of all in one people and one body".[33]

---

[31] Jamie. T. Phelps, O.P., "Communion Ecclesiology: Implications for Ecclesial and Social Transformation in the Black Catholic Community", in *Uncommon Faithfulness: The Black Catholic Experience*, ed. M. Shawn Copeland (Maryknoll, N.Y.: Orbis Books, 2009), 118–19; emphasis in original.

[32] *CCC* 813, quoting Vatican II, Decree on Ecumenism *Unitatis Redintegratio* (November 21, 1964), no. 2.

[33] *CCC* 813, quoting *Gaudium et Spes*, no. 78.

Humans are by nature relational beings because we image God, who exists in an eternal relationship of self-giving love and communion. Therefore, the Church, which is a sign and instrument of God to humanity, must, at its core, be relational. The Church invites us into covenant relationship with God and fosters solidarity among her members. The *Catechism of the Catholic Church* emphasizes that "it is the Holy Spirit, dwelling in those who believe and pervading and ruling over the entire Church, who brings about that wonderful communion of the faithful and joins them together so intimately in Christ that he is the principle of the Church's unity."[34]

The Church is one and diverse. She is one because she is the single Body of Christ, and she is diverse because she is made up of every culture, people, race, and ethnicity. The Church supports diversity because she is essentially universal without being uniform. The *Catechism* continues: "This one Church has been marked by a great *diversity* which comes from both the variety of God's gifts and the diversity of those who receive them. Within the unity of the People of God, a multiplicity of peoples and cultures is gathered together."[35] The unity and diversity in the Church share a common originating reference: God's Trinitarian life; hence, the oneness and distinction of the Church is rooted in the oneness and distinction of the Persons in the Trinity that in no way divides the single nature of God. In distinction there is no division, and their distinction is an expression of their unity and intrinsic oneness of the shared divinity.

This unity and diversity of God is the basis for the unity and the diversity of the Church. Christ established and sustained the Church on earth as a visible organization through

---

[34] *CCC* 813, quoting *Unitatis Redintegratio*, no. 2.
[35] *CCC* 814; emphasis in original.

which He communicates grace and truth to all men and women. This unity is intrinsic because of the dynamic of Christ reconciling humanity to God in His Person, thereby creating oneness among the members of His Body.

Among the challenges to solidarity in communion, Dr. Phelps states that

> we need to examine and respond constructively to the fragmentation, division, and conflict that obscure the intent of the national black Catholic movements and the mission of parishes in each diocese.... We need to construct bridges of collaboration to overcome the walls of racial and ethnic-cultural divisions.[36]

Dr. Phelps goes on to describe "fragmentation, division, and conflict" in the black Catholic community as capitulation to the moral relativism and rugged individualism of the secular culture, exchanging the Gospel for personal power and prestige, and subsequently hindering the social justice work of the Church.

Although Dr. Phelps' interesting observation was not directed toward BLM, I would say that it is definitely applicable here. Solidarity in communion with the Church is ruptured by BLM, who are using "fragmentation, division, and conflict" (the language of CRT and liberation theology) to push their radical agenda, according to their 2020 "About" web page, "to dismantle cisgender privilege and uplift Black trans folk, especially Black trans women", and to free women from family "environments in which men are centered" in order to "disrupt the Western-prescribed nuclear family structure ... with the intention of freeing ourselves from the tight grip of heteronormative

---

[36] Phelps, "Communion Ecclesiology", 119–20.

thinking." This biased framework, under the auspices of "social justice", is incompatible with Church teaching. In an attempt to uphold the inherent dignity of every human person, which is a great good, the BLM movement is actually working to refashion the Church into its image and likeness built upon the shifting sands of contemporary cultural dogma.

Dr. Phelps' second comment regarding the "need to construct bridges of collaboration to overcome the walls of racial and ethnic-cultural divisions" should be well received and encouraged. However, there is nothing in the BLM mission that speaks of dialoguing with anyone who does not share their perspective or accept their agenda. According to their most recent "About" section on their website,

> We are a collective of liberators who believe in an inclusive and spacious movement. We also believe that in order to win and bring as many people with us along the way, we must move beyond the narrow nationalism that is all too prevalent in Black communities. We must ensure we are building a movement that brings all of us to the front.[37]

Where is space for engagement and dialogue with those, like myself, who do not share the BLM vision but are working toward justice and equity for all? Dr. Phelps asserts that "the invisible unity created and maintained by our shared participation in the creative, redemptive, and sanctifying grace of God must become a visible sacrament of unity in a divided world. Personal and institutional

---

[37] Black Lives Matter website, "About" page, accessed January 10, 2023, https://blacklivesmatter.com/about/.

conversion rooted in deep contemplative prayer and discernment is the only path to such radical unity."[38] This is solidarity in communion at work. This is how we work together to make black lives matter.

Solidarity with the Gospel means that a true commitment to creating racial equality is inseparable from the Gospel *kerygma*. Jesus taught,

> Love your enemies, do good to those who hate you, bless those who curse you, pray for those who abuse you. To him who strikes you on the cheek, offer the other also; and from him who takes away your cloak do not withhold your coat as well.... And as you wish that men would do to you, do so to them. If you love those who love you, what credit is that to you? For even sinners love those who love them. And if you do good to those who do good to you, what credit is that to you? For even sinners do the same.... But love your enemies, and do good ... and your reward will be great, and you will be sons of the Most High; for he is kind to the ungrateful and the selfish. Be merciful, even as your Father is merciful.[39]

> But I say to you, Love your enemies and pray for those who persecute you, so that you may be sons of your Father who is in heaven; for he makes his sun rise on the evil and on the good, and sends rain on the just and on the unjust. For if you love those who love you, what reward have you? Do not even the tax collectors do the same? And if you salute only your brethren, what more are you doing than others? Do not even the Gentiles do the same? You, therefore, must be perfect, as your heavenly Father is perfect.[40]

[38] Phelps, "Communion Ecclesiology", 123.
[39] Lk 6:27–29, 31–33, 35–36.
[40] Mt 5:44–48.

Pray then like this:

> Our Father who art in heaven,
> Hallowed be thy name.
> Thy kingdom come.
> Thy will be done,
> On earth as it is in heaven.
> Give us this day our daily bread;
> And forgive us our trespasses,
> As we forgive those who trespass against us;
> And lead us not into temptation,
> But deliver us from evil.

> For if you forgive men their trespasses, your heavenly
> Father also will forgive you; but if you do not forgive
> men their trespasses, neither will your Father forgive your
> trespasses.[41]

Where is the BLM call for peace, reconciliation, forgiveness, and mercy? These enduring characteristics of Christian faith are nonnegotiable because they are given to us by God Himself. Any meaningful discourse with BLM must include these aspects at some level. Sadly, it appears that BLM, as Bishop Braxton observes, "does not embrace traditional Christian theological ideas about praying to keep peace and change hearts".[42]

In the final analysis, we are left with more questions than answers. If black lives really mattered, why is BLM silent regarding Planned Parenthood, an organization that kills hundreds of thousands of black lives every year? What is the BLM plan for economic growth, stability, and development in black neighborhoods? What is their plan to end drug and gang violence? Where is their plan to strengthen families? Where is their plan to create greater

---

[41] Mt 6:9–15.
[42] Braxton, "Catholic Church and Black Lives Matter Movement", 50.

educational opportunities so black children can leave their failing schools to go to the school of their choice to excel academically? What is their plan to promote black entrepreneurship? What is their plan to actually end racism?

In the face of the challenges confronting people of color today, combating only *specific aspects* of prevailing material, philosophical, and spiritual errors without working to deconstruct the *comprehensive framework* that supports and undergirds the entire corrupt structure that is rooted in sin will render any long-term, permanent solutions weak and ineffective.

The Catholic response is twofold: to work toward peace, reconciliation, forgiveness, and mercy while, at the same time, striving diligently to replace prejudiced and racist ideologies with a holistic Christian anthropology rooted in the truth, goodness, and beauty of God's law written on our hearts. Bishop Braxton comes to the conclusion that "this requires that we open our hearts to the purifying power of the Holy Spirit and the healing grace of Christ. This is the path that leads to true conversion. This means practicing the Law of Love with ourselves, our family members, our neighbors, our fellow parishioners, our co-workers.... This lifelong process will be more effective in all aspects about lives if we are faithful to the imperatives: Listen! Learn! Think! Pray! Act!"[43]

This is how we work together to make black lives matter.

---

[43] Bishop Edward K. Braxton, "Old Wounds Revisited", in *Church and Racial Divide*, 87.

CHAPTER SIX

A Catholic Response to Racism

The solution to what we are seeing and experiencing in this country regarding race is not rioting, looting, and vandalism. It is not "Christianizing" secular approaches, methods, or ideas. Overcoming racial inequality will not be accomplished by incorporating bad theology. Racism is learned behavior, and Catholics can play a significant, proactive role in breaking down the walls of racism by taking a "hands on" approach to creating pillars of mutual respect and understanding, rooted in the dignity of the human person and built on the firm foundation of a covenant relationship.

The crisis of race can be partially attributed to a leadership vacuum in society. In the 1950s and 1960s, towering figures such as Dr. Martin Luther King, Jr., led the way in raising awareness of and combatting against racial injustice. Dr. King was able to cut through the polemics of racial and socio-political division and to unite people of all races in one collective voice working peacefully together to effect change. Today, there is no such voice. In the midst of this leadership void, a number of organizations and individuals, with agendas that have nothing to do with race, are clamoring to make their voices heard. These entities are grabbing the attention of the media and making headlines, and the general public is left to form their opinions and belief systems based on what is being subjectively presented to them on mainstream and social media. These secular perspectives not only inhibit efforts to ameliorate racism effectively but actually make things worse.

In juxtaposition, the Catholic Church is perfectly situated to exercise global leadership in the struggle against the evil of racism. The Second Vatican Council's document *Gaudium et Spes* notes that "every type of discrimination, whether social or cultural ... is to be overcome and eradicated as contrary to God's intent.... The Church can anchor the dignity of human nature against all tides of opinion.... By no human law can the personal dignity and liberty of man be so aptly safeguarded as by the Gospel of Christ which has been entrusted to the Church."[1] Catholics can and must take the lead in defeating racism and prejudice.

Here are five specific steps that Catholics can take (both laypersons and clergy working together) to accomplish this goal: (1) see past stereotypes and see people, (2) appreciate the gift of cultural diversity, (3) promote conversation and dialogue, (4) put God back into society, and (5) pray constantly.

See Past Stereotypes and See People

Racist ideologies create images that leave negative impressions on susceptible and vulnerable minds and hearts, especially those of children. We need to recognize our own prejudices or racist attitudes, acknowledging them then working hard to crucify these ways of thinking. The key to defeating prejudice and racism is to see our brothers and sisters as God sees us—to look at one another through

---

[1] Vatican Council II, Pastoral Constitution on the Church in the Modern World *Gaudium et Spes* (December 7, 1965), nos. 29, 41, https://www.vatican.va/archive/hist_councils/ii_vatican_council/documents/vat-ii_const_19651207_gaudium-et-spes_en.html.

God's eyes. We need to see the image and likeness of God in one another.

The Book of Genesis says, "Then God said, 'Let us make man in our image, after our likeness.' ... So God created man in his own image, in the image of God he created him; male and female he created them."[2] In its reflection on this passage, the St. Paul Center for Biblical Theology notes that "in the language of the Bible, to be born in someone's 'image and likeness,' means to be that person's child. The expression 'image and likeness' expresses the Father-son relationship of God and His people (see Genesis 5:1–3; Luke 3:38). From the very beginning, then, we see that God intended people to be His children, His divine offspring."[3]

The word for "image" in Genesis 1:26 (צֶלֶם, *tselem*) means a shadow that is the outline or representation of the original. When there is light, our physical bodies cast a shadow that is an outline of our bodies and that moves as we move. God is pure Spirit, and His light casts the shadow of His love onto our souls. Just as our shadows move when we move, when we speak, think, and love, in cooperation with the light of grace in our souls, we reflect God's goodness in our actions.

Similarly, the word for "likeness" in the same verse (דְמוּת, *demut*) means "similar" or "resemblance". "Likeness" in this context does not mean physical similarity. If I were situated between my son and a statue of myself, one might say they both resemble me; in fact, the statue would look more like me than my son would. Unlike the statue that is lifeless, my son and I, though separate individuals, share a common human nature composed of body and

[2] Gen 1:26–27.
[3] St. Paul Center for Biblical Theology, "Covenant Love, Lesson 2.3", under "The Child-Like Image of Man", accessed January 12, 2020, https://stpaulcenter.com/covenant-love-lesson-2-3/.

soul. Consequently, my son is much more in my likeness, in the sense used in Genesis, than the statue. Since God is pure Spirit, we bear a spiritual similarity to God, who has filled us with the breath of His divine life.

Seeing every man and woman as an icon of the *imago Dei* (the image of God) is a fitting response to God's familial invitation to love and communion—to see the image and likeness of God in every person regardless of race. This speaks to the meaning of the last verse of Genesis 2: "And the man and his wife were both naked, and were not ashamed."[4] Looking upon the beauty of God's creative activity manifested in their physical bodies—in complete vulnerability before God and each other—the man and woman experience the *imago Dei*: they see each other the way God sees them. They look upon each other through God's eyes. These are the eyes through which we must see and experience our brothers and sisters of different races and colors. If we do not start with the *imago Dei*, then we will end up hopelessly spinning our wheels in attempting to remove racial barriers.

A few years ago, I spoke at a large Midwest conference. I wore a suit and tie with my Miraculous Medal and crucifix medallions around my neck, and a deacon lapel pin on my suit jacket. I arrived at the elevator to go up to my room to change, and when the doors opened, the only other occupant was a petite Caucasian woman. As I entered the elevator, I looked at her, smiled, and nodded my head to acknowledge her without saying a word. As her eyes grew wide, she took a few quick steps to the back of the elevator and clutched her purse close to her body. I knew she was afraid, so without saying anything I turned and faced the elevator doors and pushed the button for my

4 Gen 2:25.

floor. I did not turn around to look at or recognize her in any way. When I got to my floor, I stepped off the elevator and went to my room.

I completely understand that there may have been mitigating factors that contributed to her reaction. This woman could have been assaulted in the past and is suffering from post-traumatic stress syndrome, and her response was simply a reflection of that circumstance. I also understand the nervous anxiety of being in a confined space with a stranger. Fear and nervousness are one thing, grabbing your purse and pulling it to your body while physically moving away from a person is something else. I gave her no reason to be leery of me, yet she was still frightened. This is not the first time something like this has happened to me, and I am sure other people of color have had similar experiences. I can say unequivocally that it truly hurts— and hurts deeply—when people do not see the *imago Dei* in you, but only a caricature or a subconsciously projected stereotype. This is the first brick that must be removed in the wall of racism.

When we start seeing the image of God and not color as the preeminent defining characteristic of persons, then we can truly begin to appreciate each individual's unique gifts—their ethnicity and cultural diversity—that they share with the world. Catholics leading the way of *imago Dei* will be the catalysts of the yet unrealized dream of the Reverend Dr. Martin Luther King, Jr.: that all Americans "will one day live in a nation where they will not be judged by the color of their skin but by the content of their character".[5]

[5] Martin Luther King, Jr., "I Have a Dream" Speech, at the "March on Washington", 1963 (abridged), Gilder Lehrman Institute of American History, https://www.gilderlehrman.org/sites/default/files/inline-pdfs/Abridged%20 MLK%20Dream%20Speech_0.pdf. Reprinted by arrangement with the Heirs to the Estate of Martin Luther King, Jr.

God exists as a family, as a communion of Persons. The *imago Dei* means that the human family on earth is made in the image and likeness of the divine family of heaven. The realization of the kingdom of God on earth is the hermeneutic of an apostolic community's lived experience of the *imago Dei*. The International Theological Commission notes that "while affirming the fundamentally social character of human existence, Christian civilization has nonetheless recognized the absolute value of the human person as well as the importance of individual rights and cultural diversity.... The Church is the sacrament of salvation and of the kingdom of God ... in bringing together man of every race and culture [and] in being the vanguard of the unity of the human community willed by God."[6]

The kingdom of heaven has far less to do with the future than with our life in the world here and now. To be in the kingdom is to be living one's life under God's providence and guidance with absolute confidence in His merciful love. The covenant exchange of loving intimacy between creature and Creator becomes the template for effecting the greatest commandments: loving God and our neighbor as ourselves.[7] The "kingdom" means to be in a relationship of loving surrender to God's will and to create an environment on earth where true Gospel values prevail. Relationship in community rooted in the *imago Dei* speaks to the personal commitment of every individual, with all of his heart, soul, mind, and strength, to seek the face of the Lord sincerely in the person standing in front of them. This approach will lead to personal transformation

---

[6] International Theological Commission, *Communion and Stewardship: Human Persons Created in the Image of God* (July 23, 2004), nos. 42–43, https://www.vatican.va/roman_curia/congregations/cfaith/cti_documents/rc_con_cfaith_doc_20040723_communion-stewardship_en.html.

[7] See Mt 22:37–39; Mk 12:30–31; Lk 10:27.

and, consequently, the transformation of society and the inevitable implosion of racism. On this issue, preeminent Catholic scholar Hans Urs von Balthasar says, "For only in this act of self-transcending love can two things happen at once: the founding of the person and the founding of community. By opting to love,... the heart allows holiness, and holy community too, to take root within it."[8]

To this end, we must stop supporting media outlets, individuals, and organizations that create, encourage, and perpetuate racist stereotypes, or who propose violence and anarchy as solutions. This destroys community, disfigures the *imago Dei*, and discourages peaceful means to resolve differences.

Saint Paul says in Ephesians, "For he is our peace, who has made us both one, and has broken down the dividing wall of hostility."[9] Reflecting on this passage, the *Ignatius Catholic Study Bible* states that "the peace of Christ is not worldly tranquility but a spiritual peace rooted in our reconciliation with the Father."[10] This reconciliation comes by breaking down walls of enmity.[11] The *Ignatius Catholic Study Bible* further states that the "dividing wall" that Saint Paul references in the above verse from Ephesians "is alluding to a wall in the Jerusalem Temple that separated the outer court of the Gentiles from the inner courts, where Israel alone could pray and sacrifice".[12] Any Gentile trespassing into the inner courts would be put to death.

---

[8] Hans Urs von Balthasar, *You Crown the Year with Your Goodness: Sermons through the Liturgical Year* (San Francisco: Ignatius Press, 1989), 214.

[9] Eph 2:14.

[10] *Ignatius Catholic Study Bible: The New Testament; Revised Standard Version, Second Catholic Edition*, ed. Scott Hahn and Curtis Mitch (San Francisco: Ignatius Press, 2010), 347.

[11] "Hostility" is translated as "hatred" (אֵיבָה) in Hebrew. See Gen 3:15.

[12] *Ignatius Catholic Study Bible: New Testament*, 347.

The wall of separation represents the Old Testament practice of segregation that required Israel to be insulated from the idolatry and immorality of the pagan nations around them. As it states in Leviticus, "'You shall inherit their land, and I will give it to you to possess, a land flowing with milk and honey.' I am the LORD your God, who have separated you from the peoples.... You shall be holy to me; for I the LORD am holy, and have separated you from the peoples, that you should be mine."[13] Jesus breaks down the wall of separation by abolishing the law with its commandments and legal claims that set Israel apart from the Gentiles. In doing so, Christ did not demolish the *moral* law (the Ten Commandments) but the *ritual* laws and its precepts (e.g., circumcision, animal sacrifice, dietary laws, and festival days). In this way, all nations and races are united under Christ.

We will begin to see the *imago Dei* when each of us, strengthened by God's grace, remove walls of division in our own hearts. Then with hearts that are humble and contrite, and through our steadfast conviction and countercultural witness to the Gospel, we can demolish barriers of hate and ignorance by becoming living testaments to Christ's merciful love.

Living in love means we must participate deeply in Christ's vulnerability on the Cross—in the immolation of sin and the pouring forth of our true identity as sons and daughters unified by His blood. Sanctified by the grace of the Eucharistic Mystery, our evangelism will flow freely into a broken world. As the earth drinks its fill of our self-gift, sating a ground thirsting for truth with the waters of mutual respect and trust, we become co-creators with God in the *imago Dei* by building up

[13] Lev 20:24, 26.

integrated, multicultural communities that foster true peace. This "peace of God", Saint Paul says in Philippians, "which passes all understanding, will keep your hearts and your minds in Christ Jesus."[14]

Appreciate the Gift of Cultural Diversity

Cultural diversity (that is, the possession by our brothers and sisters of rich and diverse cultural heritages such as African, Asian, Caribbean, Hispanic, and Native American) can be a source of contention and volatility in parishes. Sometimes we fear what we do not understand or simply choose to ignore people who are different from us. This may cause us to put spiritual blinders on, creating a cultural tunnel vision. This may cause us to believe, for example, that Mass in Spanish is only for Hispanics, or that the Vietnamese Mass is only for Vietnamese Catholics.

As a result, tensions can make their way into parish life, causing both subtle and overt divisions within the Body of Christ. We create cultural silos and remain in the comfort zone of people who look like us. This isolation causes subtle separation from others in the parish and, if it continues, can lead to division—that is, the *perception* that one cultural group seems to be favored or preferred over another. Thus, we miss opportunities to learn from one another, to grow in God's love, and to see the image and likeness of God in the person sitting next to us in the pew. We are not loving our neighbor as ourselves.

And yet, change is possible if we are willing to work together for forgiveness, reconciliation, and peace. This role is particularly suited to the deacon. Deacons can serve

[14] Phil 4:7.

as catalysts for such change by acting as liaisons between cultural groups. By working to improve cultural appreciation and awareness, deacons can facilitate the process of healing division.

Here are a few suggestions that you can adapt and implement in your parish.

Host a series of parish potlucks. Host potlucks where each of the ethnic communities is appreciated and celebrated. The diversity of food, music, native dress, dancing, etc., can be an incredible opportunity to learn and grow. It is no mistake that in the Gospels Jesus can often be found eating at someone's house. The Lord accepted the invitation of all: tax collectors, sinners, and Pharisees. Food and hospitality were important vehicles used by Jesus to bring disparate groups together. Sharing a meal became an important way to share the faith.

During the potlucks, have a few parishioners of color, or those with diverse ethnic backgrounds, share stories and short testimonies of their experience of being in the Catholic Church. Other parishioners will begin to realize how much they all have in common and, slowly but surely, the parish family will come closer together.

A wonderfully creative example of how the potluck model was implemented prior to the Covid pandemic was at Our Lady of Dolours Catholic Parish in Chatswood (Sydney), Australia.[15] The parish has a program called "Eat, Pray & Chill" that operates three Thursdays each month. They have a food truck featuring meals from Malaysia, Philippines, and Singapore. After the meal, the parishioners head to the church for Eucharistic Adoration. Afterward, there

---

[15] "Eat, Pray, & Chill", accessed December 15, 2021, https://www.bbcatholic.org.au/chatswood/ministries/community-dinners.

is an opportunity to eat again, this time with entertainment provided by a parishioner who plays the guitar and sings.

Potlucks may seem basic and unsophisticated, but there is a beautiful simplicity and homogeneity in this approach, which is precisely why it is effective. No formal programming, extensive planning, or committees are required: just families sharing a meal and conversing around the dinner table, which is a natural extension of sharing the Eucharist as a family at the Holy Sacrifice of the Mass. Again, deacons, as icons of Christ the Servant, can play a key role in organizing these.

If you do not have much cultural diversity in your parish, not to worry. You can invite Catholics of color from neighboring parishes. The potluck is a simple and fun way to begin removing stereotypes and caricatures, and to start seeing people.

Have choirs from each ethnic group occasionally lead singing at other Masses. If your parish has cultural Masses (e.g., Creole, Vietnamese, Hispanic, or Nigerian), have the choirs from each ethnic group occasionally lead the singing at the other Masses—for example, the Vietnamese choir at the English Mass, the Hispanic choir at the Creole Mass, the English choir at the Nigerian Mass, and so forth. The parishioners may experience culture shock at first—and even offer resistance and criticism—but over time they will begin to appreciate the authentic and reverent cultural expressions that acknowledge the unique gifts we all bring to the Holy Sacrifice of the Mass and the entire Body of Christ.[16]

---

[16] If you decide to implement this in your parish, please ensure that you supply song sheets with the printed lyrics, even if they are not in English. The last thing you want is for people to feel like they are at a concert. Even if they do not understand the words, they can still follow along. Having a parallel English translation would be optimal.

I want to emphasize "authentic and reverent cultural expressions". Music can be a source of contention in parishes. It has been my experience that parishioners will make decisions on which Sunday Mass (and in some cases, which parish) they attend based on how reverently the Mass is celebrated, which includes the style of music sung by the choir. I understand and can sympathize with the fact that some music at Mass feels like entertainment and not worship that honors God.

The teaching of the Church on inculturation in the Mass is clear. The Apostolic See and, in some cases, the episcopal conference and the local bishop have sole authority to determine how liturgical rites are celebrated. The Congregation for Divine Worship and the Discipline of the Sacraments, quoting the Second Vatican Council document on the liturgy, *Sacrosanctum Concilium*, notes that "'no other person, not even if he is a priest, may on his own initiative add, remove or change anything in the liturgy.' Inculturation is not left to the personal initiative of celebrants or to the collective initiative of an assembly."[17] This directive ensures that reverence, not innovation, is the order of the day in liturgical celebrations.

Secular music and dance has no place in the Mass. In the Sacred Liturgy, heaven and earth meet. We leave our secular lives behind for a time and enter the realm of divine worship. As the Congregation for Divine Worship and the Discipline of the Sacraments teaches:

> Music and singing, which express the soul of people, have pride of place in the liturgy. And so singing must be promoted, in the first place singing the liturgical text, so that

[17] Congregation for Divine Worship and the Discipline of the Sacraments, Instruction: Inculturation and the Roman Liturgy (March 29, 1994), no. 37, https://www.ewtn.com/catholicism/library/instruction-inculturation-and -the-roman-liturgy-2180. Internal quote is from *Sacrosanctum Concilium*, no. 22.

the voices of the faithful may be heard in the liturgical actions themselves. . . .

Musical forms, melodies and musical instruments could be used in divine worship as long as they "are suitable, or can be made suitable, for sacred use, and provided they are in accord with the dignity of the place of worship and truly contribute to the uplifting of the faithful" (*Sacrosanctum Concilium*, no. 120).[18]

The major objection with inculturation and music at Mass that causes the most angst is the variety of unique cultural expressions that occur while singing: rhythmic swaying, clapping hands, and dance-like movements. These are often seen as irreverent but, in many cultures, are actually forms of prayer and joy-filled articulations of worship. "Such forms of external expression," the Congregation for Divine Worship and the Discipline of the Sacraments says, "can have a place in the liturgical actions of these peoples on condition that they are always the expression of true communal prayer of adoration, praise, offering and supplication, and not simply a performance."[19] This will undoubtedly require parishioners to be informed and educated on how cultural expressions are truly liturgical in nature. This effort is yet another small but significant step forward toward closing the racial divide.

Add multicultural images of saints in the church. There is no reason why parishes cannot have statues, pictures, and icons of saints of color like Martin de Porres, Kateri Tekakwitha, and Juan Diego, as well as cultural images of Mary—for example, Our Lady of La Vang. Although more subtle, these sacred images counterbalance negative secular images and stereotypes.

[18] Ibid., no. 40.
[19] Ibid., no. 42.

A simple example will illustrate the point. Imagine a third-grader who walks into his predominately Caucasian church for Sunday Mass that has very few, if any, people of color in attendance. He sees images of black, Hispanic, and Asian saints in the narthex, vestibule, or gathering space. Having never seen a saint of color, he stops in front of one of images and asks his dad, "Who is that?" His father smiles and says, "That is Saint Josephine Bakhita," and, in an age-appropriate way, explains the importance of this great saint. These sublime images have provided a powerful and positive counternarrative to the negative portrayals of people of color that he may have been exposed to, and they have opened his eyes to the rich cultural diversity found within the Catholic Church.

When you enter someone's home, you will most likely see pictures of family members and loved ones, sometimes going back generations: parents, children, grandparents, great grandparents, cousins, and so forth. They are family members that are remembered and celebrated with loving affection. The parish church is our home, and our fellow parishioners on earth and the saints in heaven are the members of our family. Why wouldn't we honor those family members who have gone before us by displaying their images throughout the parish? This is a very simple way to make Catholics of color feel welcomed.

Promote Conversation and Dialogue

Back in 2016, celebrity rappers Snoop Dogg (Calvin Broadus) and the Game (Jayceon Terrell Taylor) organized a summit where they met with the Los Angeles police chief and mayor. The purpose was to facilitate effective change through dialogue and understanding. Efforts like this need to be applauded and multiplied, where communication barriers are shattered and respectful dialogue is opened between Catholics of various racial and cultural backgrounds.

One of the easiest ways to do this is to form parish study groups to discuss Church documents on racism. These groups can meet once or twice a month, working through each document thoughtfully and prayerfully. Study groups like these can also be an excellent form of mystagogy for new Catholics who have entered the Church through the RCIA process and are looking to go deeper in their faith. Again, deacons can serve as excellent facilitators of these groups.

Here are a few documents to consider:

Congregation for Divine Worship and the Discipline of the Sacraments, Instruction: Inculturation and the Roman Liturgy (March 29, 1994)

Cyprian Davis, O.S.B., *The History of Black Catholics in the United States* (New York: Crossroad Publishing, 1990)

Joseph L. Howze et al., *"What We Have Seen and Heard": A Pastoral Letter on Evangelization from the Black Bishops of the United States* (Cincinnati: St. Anthony Messenger Press, 1984)

National Conference of Catholic Bishops, Committee on African American Catholics, *Love Thy Neighbor As Thyself: U.S. Catholic Bishops Speak Against Racism; January 1997–June 2000* (Washington, D.C.: United States Catholic Conference, 2001)

National Conference of Catholic Bishops, Committee on African American Catholics, *Keep Your Hand on the Plow: The African American Presence in the Catholic Church* (Washington, D.C.: United States Catholic Conference, 1996)

United States Conference of Catholic Bishops, Committee on Cultural Diversity in the Church, *Open Wide Our Hearts: The Enduring Call to Love; A Pastoral Letter against Racism* (Washington, D.C.: United States Conference of Catholic Bishops, 2018)

Pontifical Commission for Justice and Peace, *The Church and Racism: Towards a More Fraternal Society* (November 3, 1988)

International Theological Commission, *Communion and Stewardship: Human Persons Created in the Image of God* (July 23, 2004)

National Black Catholic Congress XII, *Pastoral Plan of Action* (November 27, 2017)

The biggest challenge will be getting study groups started. This may be difficult for a number of reasons: lack of interest and desire, little or no support, excuses (e.g., "We already have too much going on"), and busyness with families, jobs, and everyday life. Some people will not come to the study group because they believe racism and prejudice do not exist, or they do not want to miss the football game, or they simply do not think about these issues at all. No matter. As the saying goes, "The longest journey starts with a single step." The study group is not about metrics and large numbers of participants, but the glorification of God. As Psalm 37 says, "Commit your way to the LORD; trust in him, and he will act."[20]

Honest conversation, where people feel comfortable and encouraged to speak openly, should be a priority. For example, I would very much welcome a discussion where someone asked, "I'm not sure why, but when I'm around

---

[20] Ps 37:5 in *The Liturgy of the Hours*, vol. 3, Ordinary Time, Weeks 1–17 (New York: Catholic Book Publishing, 1975), 759.

people of color I don't know, I feel afraid. It doesn't make any sense, and I don't want to feel this way. Can we talk about it?" The beauty of this question lies not only in its vulnerability but in the person's desire to understand, grow, and change. These are the initial steps on the journey to racial equality rooted in the *imago Dei*.

Deep-seated commitments to building integrity, sharing wisdom, and imparting knowledge can lead to reciprocity of love and change. Reaching out with compassion to those of different races and hearing their stories, responding with empathy, and working through differences with humble, contrite hearts can create a harmonic of love that will reverberate in our hearts and throughout our land.

Put God Back into Society

When we remove God from the public square, we make room for the devil. The lawlessness, pejorative rhetoric, and constant assault on religious liberty and freedom rampant in our culture are signs of this.

Throughout history, sin has been a major obstacle to achieving true human freedom lived in God's image and likeness. The Reverend Dr. Martin Luther King, Jr., said, "So often we try to deny this fact.... We know how to love, and yet we hate. We take the precious lives that God has given us and throw them away. We are unfaithful to those to whom we should be faithful. We are disloyal to those ideals to which we should be loyal. 'We are like sheep that have gone astray.'"[21]

---

[21] Martin Luther King, Jr., *The Measure of a Man* (Philadelphia: Christian Education Press, 1959), 10, 12.

As faithful Catholics, we can no longer allow secular culture and ideology—with its promulgation of subjective, relativistic truth—to displace the objective, absolute truth of Catholic doctrine and principles. In order to defeat racism, there must be further introspection and a deeper examination of conscience in order to arrive at the root cause of the disunity and divisiveness within humanity that leads to sinful actions—where we see ourselves and worldly principles as the autonomous center of all truth.

We all live with the reality of human frailty and weakness, both within ourselves and in those we love. We must recognize and acknowledge the reality of sin—that it affects us and speaks to us within the depths of our being. Yet, we cannot allow the pain of sin and the suffering it causes to take root in our hearts. We cannot allow sin to control us, or its anguish to overwhelm us. Conquering sin in our lives begins with personal conversion—a conscious and sincere turning back toward the Lord that reveals fundamental truths of our being and existence: we are made by God to give and receive love, and to proclaim the truth in love.

Consequently, we must no longer be a Church that reacts to the dictates of the culture, allowing "wokeism", deplatforming, and virtue signaling to run roughshod over us. We must resist moral relativism and reject secular humanism. We must not be afraid to preach boldly the beauty and truth of the Gospel in love no matter the cost. We must pick up our crosses and follow Christ wherever He leads. The Scriptures fill us with confidence for the task: "The LORD is my light and my help; whom shall I fear? The Lord is the stronghold of my life; before whom shall I shrink? When -evil-doers draw near to devour my flesh, it is they, my enemies and foes, who stumble and fall."[22]

[22] Ps 27:1–2 (RSV-CE).

The secular culture does not take people of faith seriously, because we are divided. This is not God's will. Jesus prayed, "The glory which you have given me I have given to them, that they may be one even as we are one, I in them and you in me, that they may become perfectly one, so that the world may know that you have sent me and have loved them even as you have loved me."[23] Catholics must take the lead in helping to unite the Body of Christ.

The prophet Isaiah[24] predicted that at a time when the world was enveloped in darkness, the glory of the Lord would shine over Jerusalem. This heavenly light, the Light of Christ, will be a beacon to all nations. What is striking is how the visit of the Wise Men to the house in Bethlehem is similar to the experience of our own parish families, and how beautifully both the Gospel and parishes reflect the universal Church.

The Magi are typically represented as multiracial kings from the East, and our Catholic parishes are comprised of multiracial people from around the world. By the grace of the Holy Spirit and from the four corners of the earth, Catholics have left their countries of origin and followed the Lord Jesus Christ, the Light that shines in the darkness, to parishes around the globe where they offer their gifts— gold: the prosperity and riches of their time, talent, and treasure to build up the kingdom of God; frankincense: their prayers, hopes, and dreams rising to heaven and presented by the angels before the throne of Almighty God; myrrh: the offering of their lives in sacrifice and service to God and the parish family, as well as to the poor and outcast, the sick and the lonely.

[23] Jn 17:22–23.
[24] Is 60:1–6.

Let us not become so comfortable with our own lives and disinterested in the lives of others that our ears become deaf to the message of salvation, and our hearts become closed to the miracles God works in our lives every day. We still live in a world enveloped in the darkness of racial division. Let us be inspired by the faith of the Wise Men to fulfill in our lives what the Lord commands: that we may be one. Let us be filled with a faith that inspires the Holy Spirit to enliven the Father's love in our hearts. Let us open the abundant treasury of our lives and generously share our gifts by becoming living witnesses of unity in Christ to the world.

Pray Constantly

Prayer is both a gift of grace and a response that takes effort on our part. In order for us to walk humbly before our God in the obedience of faith, we must appreciate the fact that we cannot eliminate racism and prejudice on our own; we need God's help every step of the way, especially during these turbulent and troubling times. Anyone who truly believes in God's infinite love will abandon himself totally to Him in prayer and, in that complete self-gift, will find the courage to defeat the scourge of racism, discovering the peace and certainty for which his heart longs. I recommend the following.

Pray before Jesus in the Most Blessed Sacrament. Pray before Jesus in front of a tabernacle or a monstrance in Eucharistic Adoration, where He is truly, fully, and substantially present in the Most Blessed Sacrament. Pray for personal conversion as well as the strength and commitment to be a voice and advocate for real change.

Add fasting to your prayer. Many people pray, but the combination of prayer and fasting can produce powerful results. Mark says in his Gospel, "And when he had entered the house, his disciples asked him privately, 'Why could we not cast it out?' And he said to them, 'This kind cannot be driven out by anything but prayer and fasting.'"[25]

The fast can be from food and drink, or from an activity that we enjoy. Fasting is effective because the feeling of emptiness produced by the deprivation of a physical good (food, television, etc.) reminds us that what we are really seeking and hungering for—what our hearts truly desire—is a life-giving relationship with the Living God. Fasting empties us so that God can fill us.

Unite the principles of Catholic social teaching with the Beatitudes. So that faith becomes not simply "what we do" but "who we are", with a special emphasis on achieving racial equity by nurturing peace, unite the principles of Catholic social teaching with the Beatitudes (found in Matthew 5:1–12). The *Catechism of the Catholic Church* reiterates that

> respect for and development of human life require peace. Peace is not merely the absence of war, and it is not limited to maintaining a balance of powers between adversaries. Peace cannot be attained on earth without safeguarding the goods of persons, free communication among men, respect for the dignity of persons and peoples, and the assiduous practice of fraternity. Peace is "the tranquility of order" (Saint Augustine, *De Civitate Dei* [*The City of God*] 19, 13, 1). Peace is the work of justice and the effect of charity.[26]

[25] Mk 9:28–29.
[26] CCC 2304.

The key to understanding the rich blessings of the Beatitudes is acknowledging our dependence on God and saying yes to Christ's invitation to live with Him in the Father and the Holy Spirit, who ignites the flame of our love in our hearts. And since the love of God embraces all of humanity, we who follow Christ are called to share in His work of salvation in a special way. Living the Beatitudes is our response to God's divine grace in us.

Jesus says, "Blessed are the peacemakers."[27] Peacemakers help to break down the many barriers that divide people and are thus called "children of God". The Father sent His Son to break down the walls between God and His people, and sometimes even between the people themselves. In its document on Catholic social teaching regarding solidarity, the United States Conference of Catholic Bishops (USCCB) states that "we are one human family whatever our national, racial, ethnic, economic, and ideological differences. We are our brothers' and sisters' keepers, wherever they may be. Loving our neighbor has global dimensions in a shrinking world. At the core of the virtue of solidarity is the pursuit of justice and peace.... The Gospel calls us to be peacemakers. Our love for all our sisters and brothers demands that we promote peace in a world surrounded by violence and conflict."[28]

Ask for the intercession of the Blessed Virgin Mary. As Pope John Paul wrote in *Mulieris Dignitatem*, "In God's

[27] Mt 5:9.

[28] United States Conference of Catholic Bishops, "Seven Themes of Catholic Social Teaching", USCCB.org, accessed January 10, 2023, https://www.usccb.org/beliefs-and-teachings/what-we-believe/catholic-social-teaching/seven-themes-of-catholic-social-teaching. Text is from *Sharing Catholic Social Teaching: Challenges and Directions* (Washington, D.C.: USCCB, 1998) and *Faithful Citizenship: A Catholic Call to Political Responsibility* (Washington, D.C.: USCCB, 2003).

eternal plan, woman is the one in whom the order of love in the created world of persons takes first root. The order of love belongs to the intimate life of God himself, the life of the Trinity.... Through the Spirit,... love becomes a gift for created persons.... *The dignity of women is measured by the order of love*, which is essentially the order of justice and charity."[29]

Simeon prophesies that Mary's soul will be pierced through and her heart torn open by the pain of watching her only Son suffer and die.[30] The lesson for us is this: by making ourselves vulnerable before Jesus through the heart of love—through the pierced soul of the Virgin Mary—we can truly unite our hearts to the heart of Christ and make more fully ours what He has accomplished on the Cross: life-giving union with the Father.

Psalm 22, written by David, foreshadows Christ's Crucifixion but also the presence of His mother, Mary, at Calvary: "Yes, it was you who took me from the womb, entrusted me to my mother's breast. To you I was committed from my birth; from my mother's womb you have been my God. Do not leave me alone in my distress; Come close, there is none else to help."[31] There are no recorded words of Mary at the Crucifixion: Mary listened! We answer the call to transformation by listening attentively and in silence to the voice of God and allowing that voice to change our lives; it is answering the call of the Holy Spirit to be still and know that Jesus Christ is Lord.

[29] Pope John Paul II, apostolic letter *Mulieris Dignitatem* (August 15, 1988), no. 29 (emphasis in original), https://www.vatican.va/content/john-paul-ii/en/apost_letters/1988/documents/hf_jp-ii_apl_19880815_mulieris-dignitatem.html.

[30] Lk 2:34–35.

[31] Ps 22:9–11 in *The Liturgy of the Hours*, 1093.

The last words of Mary recorded in the Gospels are "Do whatever he tells you."[32] Mary points the way to Jesus. Through Mary, God wants us to know that He understands what it is like to experience great sadness and humiliation, unbelievable pain and suffering, and even the darkness of death itself. God wants us to know that we are not alone and, by becoming incarnate in the womb of Mary, shows us a human being like ourselves who, in love, humbles herself before God and opens her heart to His holy will—devoting herself completely to discipleship in Christ—and that we, too, can share in God's divine life.

Mary kept all of these things in her Immaculate Heart[33] and united her prayers to her Son's. Jesus prayed before He went to the Cross,[34] and it is precisely these dry, dark periods when we are forced to pray from a position of disillusion and anxiety that lead us into the very heart of Christ's death and Resurrection. When we pray, we ask God to lower the walls that we have erected between Him and ourselves, so that, by the power of the Holy Spirit, Jesus enters into our most guarded places willing to set us free to love.

One of the greatest weapons in our spiritual arsenal in this battle against racism is total consecration to the Blessed Virgin Mary. At Fatima, she exhorts us to "sacrifice yourselves for sinners, and say many times, especially whenever you make some sacrifice: O Jesus, it is for love of You, for the conversion of sinners, and for reparation for the sins committed against the Immaculate Heart of Mary."[35] Our Blessed Mother is a beacon of hope that pierces the dense

[32] Jn 2:5.

[33] See Lk 2:19, 51.

[34] Mt 26:36–46; Mk 14:32–42; Lk 22:40–46.

[35] John Hauf, ed., *The Message of Fatima: Lucia Speaks* (Washington, N.J.: AMI Press, 1997), 17.

fog of anxiety and trepidation, and illuminates our path to the solid rock of our faith who is Jesus Christ. All that remains, John Hauf writes, is our choice to either "accept God's love so that it can prove effective and fruitful in us, or cower in our darkness in order to evade the light of this love".[36]

The triumph of God's love through Mary's Immaculate Heart not only frees us from sin but also frees us for participation in works of mercy, thereby bringing God's light into the world. To evangelize means to bear witness in a convincing manner to the victory of God's love over the power of evil in ourselves and in the world.

We Are a People of Hope

Despite the efforts of Dr. King and the countless others who gave their hearts, souls, and lives to the cause of justice, peace, and equality, racism remains an evil that endures to this day. It is not because Dr. King failed. Racism persists in our world because of the existence of evil and sin. Dr. King understood that racism is a distortion rooted in the very heart of human nature. The bishops of the United States agree.

> Racism is not merely one sin among many; it is a radical evil that divides the human family and denies the new creation of a redeemed world. To struggle against it demands an equally radical transformation, in our own minds and hearts as well as in the structure of our society.... The ultimate remedy against evils such as [racism] will not come solely from human effort. What is needed is the recreation

[36] Ibid., 178.

of the human being according to the image revealed in Jesus Christ. For He reveals in himself what each human being can and must become.[37]

We must not be afraid to live out our baptismal call to holiness with fervor and enthusiasm! We must not be afraid to stand up for truth, justice, and peace. Let us lovingly accept our Lord's invitation to "go and do likewise"[38] as living signs and witnesses of God's tender love and mercy, so that we may truly be "the salt of the earth" and "the light of the world".[39]

This perspective is echoed beautifully in the words of Saint John Paul the Great, who addressed black Catholics in the United States with these words:

> I express *my deep love and esteem for the black Catholic community in the United States*. Its vitality is a sign of hope for society. Composed as you are of many lifelong Catholics, and many who have more recently embraced the faith, together with a growing immigrant community, you reflect the Church's ability to bring together a diversity of people united in faith, hope and love, sharing a communion with Christ in the Holy Spirit. I urge you to keep alive and active *your rich cultural gifts....* Continue to inspire us by your desire to forgive—as Jesus forgave— and by your *desire to be reconciled* with all the people of this nation, even those who would unjustly deny you the full exercise of your human rights.... It is important to realize that there is no black Church, no white Church, no American Church; but there is and must be, in the one

[37] National Conference of Catholic Bishops, *Brothers and Sisters to Us: U.S. Catholic Bishops' Pastoral Letter on Racism* (Washington, D.C.: United States Catholic Conference, 1979), https://www.usccb.org/committees/african-american -affairs/brothers-and-sisters-us.

[38] Lk 10:37.

[39] Mt 5:13–14.

Church of Jesus Christ, a home for blacks, whites, Americans, every culture and race.[40]

The Good Samaritan

To understand the power of the parable of the Good Samaritan,[41] it is important to recognize the context in which Jesus tells it.

First, a scholar of the Mosaic law tries to test Jesus by asking him a question to which he already knew the answer: "Teacher, what shall I do to inherit eternal life?"[42] Jesus does not fall for it and, employing a classic technique used by rabbis, answers the question with a question: "What is written in the law?"[43] In response, the lawyer answers his own question by quoting what Jesus would later quote and call in Matthew 22:37–39 the greatest commandments: "You shall love the Lord your God with all your heart, and with all your soul, and with all your strength, and with all your mind [quoting Deut 6:5]; and your neighbor as yourself [quoting Levi 19:18]."[44] Jesus is teaching the lawyer a moral lesson. Commenting on this passage, the *Ignatius Catholic Study Bible* states that "love for our neighbor must accompany our love for God. These together, and not one without the other, are indispensable for living in God's friendship."[45] Jesus also makes the point

---

[40] Pope John Paul II, Meeting with the Black Catholic Community of New Orleans (September 12, 1987), nos. 3, 7 (emphasis in original), https://www.vatican.va/content/john-paul-ii/en/speeches/1987/september/documents/hf_jp-ii_spe_19870912_cattolici-new-orleans.html.

[41] Lk 10:25–37.

[42] Lk 10:25.

[43] Lk 10:26.

[44] Lk 10:27.

[45] *Ignatius Catholic Study Bible: New Testament*, 129.

that "holiness as defined by the Old Covenant is now surpassed by the holiness of the New."[46]

The trip from Jerusalem to Jericho is a seventeen-mile
journey. The rough terrain made the roadway a target
area for bandits and thieves. In the parable, the priest and
the Levite, who were expected to follow the commandments, were most likely walking in the other direction
toward the Temple in Jerusalem. They carefully passed
by on the other side of the road because the injured man
would have been bleeding, and they dare not touch him
lest they defile themselves ritually and violate the Mosaic
law.[47] The priest and Levite ignored the man for religious
reasons and thought themselves justified.

Anxious to justify himself, the scholar asks Jesus for the
meaning of the word "neighbor".[48] For him "neighbor"
meant only other Jews like himself—but did Jesus mean to
include *every* Jew, even those who *did not* follow the Law?
Was he supposed to love *them* also?

The Samaritan, in the eyes of the Jews, was an alien, an
unwanted foreigner. There was strong hostility between
the two neighboring peoples. Jews and Samaritans were
ethnically related and shared some of the Jewish beliefs,
but the Samaritans were seen as heretics. In fact, they were
held in such contempt by the Jews that, in answer to Jesus'
question about which of the three men was a neighbor to
the stranger who was robbed and beaten, the lawyer could
not bring himself to answer, "The Samaritan," but only,
"The one who showed mercy on him."[49]

Yet, this despised outsider—presumed to have nothing
of the spirit of God's mercy and compassion—gives the

[46] Ibid.
[47] See Lev 21:1–3.
[48] Lk 10:29.
[49] Lk 10:37.

Jewish man lying on the ground the attention that the clerics refused to give. In fact, the Samaritan went to extraordinary lengths to take care of the injured man, sparing no
expense. The two denarii (silver coins) that the Samaritan
spent on him may not seem like very much to us today,
but it represented two days' wages and would have been
enough to cover lodging expenses until his return. What's
more, the priest and Levite did not make any humanitarian
effort to help the man all; they could have at least called for
help or let someone else know what happened.

What would you have done in that situation? It is easy
to say, in retrospect, "I would help the guy." But what if
the almost dead man was the person who raped you? Who
molested you as a child? Who drove drunk and killed your
mother? As we walk by that person on the side of the
road, the anger and hatred we feel would burn like a fire
in our hearts, and we would want—more than anything—
for that person to suffer greatly, even to the point of death.
We would want to leave him lying there and say, "You
deserve it!" and not give him a second thought.

Yet, our Lord calls us to do the seemingly impossible
by teaching that we *must* be Good Samaritans. Further
commenting on this passage, the *Ignatius Catholic Study
Bible* states that "the Samaritan exemplifies this new standard of holiness, where God no longer requires his people
to separate from others, but calls them to extend mercy to
everyone in need and to exclude no one on the grounds of
prejudice"[50] or race. Our Lord gives us no other options
and makes no exceptions.

The parable of the Good Samaritan tells the story of our
salvation and shows us the way to overcome racial divisions. The *Ignatius Catholic Study Bible* notes that Adam,

---

[50] *Ignatius Catholic Study Bible: New Testament*, 129.

who represents the fullness of humanity in Genesis, "is the man attacked by Satan and his legions; he is stripped of his immortality and left dead in sin. The priest and the Levite represent the Old Covenant and its inability to restore man to new life. Jesus Christ comes as the Good Samaritan to rescue man from death and bring him to the inn of the Church for [spiritual] refreshment and healing through the sacraments."[51] Our Lord tells us that we must love our enemies and, in the parable of the Good Samaritan, reveals the love and mercy of God and demands that Christians be guided in their lives by love and mercy toward their neighbor.[52] As Pope John Paul II says so beautifully in *Dives in Misericordia*, "Believing in the crucified Son means 'seeing the Father' (cf. Jn 14:9), means believing that love is present in the world and that this love is more powerful than any kind of evil in which individuals, humanity, or the world are involved. Believing in this love means believing in mercy."[53]

Who is the person of color you have written off and left for dead at the roadside of your life? Who is the person of color in your life who does not know the love and mercy of God? Mercy and forgiveness demonstrate the presence in the world of a love that is more powerful than sin. If we are to defeat the evil of racial injustice, we must always lead with love. Only love can completely transform the human person.

We must be the Samaritan.

[51] Ibid.

[52] See Pope John Paul II, encyclical letter *Dives in Misericordia* (Rich in Mercy) (November 30, 1980), no. 3, https://www.vatican.va/content/john -paul-ii/en/encyclicals/documents/hf_jp-ii_enc_30111980_dives-in-miseri cordia.html#-27.

[53] Ibid., no. 7.

AFTERWORD

The Story of Six Black Catholics on the Road to Sainthood

by Michael R. Heinlein

The Catholic Church in the United States is in a privileged position at this moment to take the lead on racial justice in our society. To do so, the faithful and their shepherds must keep their gazes fixed upon the Lord, who died to take away our sins and who shows how and encourages us to bear much fruit in our call to glorify the Father with Him. The Christian call is no less than to build a civilization of love—a civilization in which racism can occupy no space.

On the night before He died, Christ prayed for unity among His flock.[1] This means that He alone is our guide, not politics, agendas, or ideologies. When anything but Christ guides us, we fall prey to the one who works against Christ's will. Having died to set us free, Christ showed us how to love and live through His death. His call to "abide in my love"[2] urges us to build the civilization of love, bearing much fruit in the world as His disciples. This takes no less than the conversion of hearts, minds, and wills so that each of us will live according to the glorious truth that God makes us in His image. This call to advance the kingdom of God here and now means, among other things,

[1] Jn 17:11, 21–22.
[2] Jn 15:9.

that we work toward the day when racism will no longer maintain the grip on our culture that it has had from its earliest days.

Looking to this end, one key for success, as many of us have argued in recent years, is for the faithful to embrace the "Holy Six", the black Catholic men and women currently under formal consideration for canonization by the Church. Each of these individuals—Venerable Pierre Toussaint, Venerable Henriette DeLille, Venerable Augustus Tolton, and Servants of God Mary Lange, Julia Greeley, and Thea Bowman—dwelled in Christ's love and reflected it amid a broken world.

The witness of each is a manifestation of Saint Paul's recognition that "where sin increased, grace abounded all the more"[3]—specifically, in the midst and aftermath of slavery's invasive, hideous hold on America, and in the related prevalence of racist thinking and behavior that has dominated American culture since its earliest days. Now is the time for all in the Church to recognize these Holy Six as heroes of the faith, and to work actively to promote their stories, foster devotion to them, and see to it that their causes of canonization advance. That was the primary motivation behind my book *Black Catholics on the Road to Sainthood*,[4] which was the first to gather the biographies of all six in one place. Each biography is accompanied by a reflection from a diverse assembly of notable contemporary Catholics. While the stories of the Holy Six are told more fully in that volume, I'm honored to reflect here upon how the witness of each of them inspires and challenges us as we seek to respond to the threats and effects of racism. Since

[3] Rom 5:20.
[4] Michael R. Heinlein, ed., *Black Catholics on the Road to Sainthood* (Huntington, Ind.: Our Sunday Visitor, 2021).

the holiness and discipleship of the Holy Six draw us more deeply into the mystery of Christ's saving love, we need their witness to show us the way forward.

Faith, Hope, and Charity

The world needs the abiding faith and indomitable trust in God that we find in the life of Mother Mary Lange. While we do not know the history of her own vocational discernment, it is clear that Lange was unable to pronounce religious vows for some time because of the color of her skin. Not a few Catholics at the time refused to believe that "colored" women should be permitted to wear the habit of a nun, and no convent would accept them either. She bided her time, praying and longing for the day in which she could become a consecrated woman, doing the work God placed before her, particularly in operating a free school out of her home.

Through pain and humiliation, Lange grew in her dependence on God's providence and intensified in her obedience to his call. Eventually, in 1829, God provided a way for Lange to offer her gifts and talents to the Church and society as a religious woman when Sulpician Father James Joubert invited her and three companions to be inaugural members of a new religious congregation to staff a school at his Baltimore parish. The Oblate Sisters of Providence were born, the first successful congregation in the United States for African American women. Although Lange had finally found her place within the Church, she was not free from racism's grip on society, even in the Church. But she believed that, in God's time, and supported by her own silent suffering, a better day would come for the Church when women like her would not have to suffer as she did.

Icons of hope like Julia Greeley, who will not be hardened by the fear and darkness that can come with the sorrows and pain of life, are so desperately needed today. While the laws of society meant that Greeley was enslaved for the first half of her life, a beautiful freedom rose up from her heart, for she knew that her Redeemer lives. After the laws changed and Greeley was allowed to live in the freedom God bestows on us all, she left behind the pain of Missouri and made her way to Denver. Like Christ, while her life never amounted to much in the eyes of the world, Greeley's love and generosity spread like a fire. Greeley took upon herself the work of a chapter of the Society of St. Vincent de Paul or a local office of Catholic Charities, financed by whatever meager income she made from odd jobs. She traversed Denver's streets pulling a red wagon filled with items for the needy she encountered. Greeley knew the truth of what it meant to gain by giving, and it showed. At her funeral in 1918, more than a thousand people came to usher her into eternal life. A longtime encourager of devotion to the Sacred Heart of Jesus, Greeley was a living embodiment of what Christ's heart brings to the world. Like her, we must turn to the Sacred Heart, which, as the litany states, is the "salvation of those who hope" in Christ, "our peace and reconciliation".

The love of Christ's heart shone brightly in the life of Pierre Toussaint, and the world needs more like him. While some criticize him for not being an activist in a society that would have punished him greatly, or for not buying or accepting his freedom earlier, having been brought to New York City as a slave, Toussaint appears to have been crafty enough to make use of the system he was thrust into to effect real change in the lives of real people. Employed as a hairdresser, Toussaint had access to the rich and famous in New York—a lucrative position at that time. But that does not mean he was immune to racism. Toussaint was once turned away at the door of a church—the construction of which he had helped finance—because of his race. His race also dictated that he must walk past public transportation as he made his way to Mass each morning. But Toussaint was not embittered; instead, he was emboldened to show more love to a world in need of it. Not concerned about storing up treasure for himself, Toussaint used the sizable income received as a coiffeur to fund an impressive and extensive charitable outreach to the poor and marginalized in his midst. He bought freedom of slaves, took in boarders and orphans, ran a credit bureau and a makeshift employment agency, helped build orphanages and churches, and opened hostels for refugees and clergy. When asked, in 1853 on his deathbed, if he needed anything, he replied, "Nothing on earth."[5] Such was a man who had Christ in his heart and who shared him with the world.

Fidelity and Loyalty to the Church

Critics of the Church sometimes cite the stories of Henriette DeLille and Augustus Tolton as evidence that the Church is systemically racist. As Deacon Harold pointed out in his text, however, it is not the Church herself that is sinful, but her members. The fact that, because of the color of their skin, Tolton was rejected from American seminaries and DeLille was not admitted to any convents in New Orleans meant that individuals in the Church, and even structures in place at that time in society and in the

[5] Literally "Rien sur la terre." Hannah Farnham Sawyer Lee, *Memoir of Pierre Toussaint, Born a Slave in St. Domingo* (Boston: Crosby, Nichols and Co., 1854), 113.

Church, were sinful. But nothing in the Church's teaching justified such decisions. In the face of these criticisms, we look to the examples of Tolton and DeLille themselves, both of whom possessed an undying perseverance in the love for Christ and the Church. Despite any obstacles they faced, they boldly sought to offer their lives in service to the Gospel. Knowing the Church was truly Christ's Body, they fought and persevered for it in spite of the sinful men and women who manipulated it to sinful ends.

The Church, and the wider society, needs someone like Tolton, who worked tirelessly for unity and reconciliation, particularly in the face of a great deal of division and hatred. Tolton had to travel to Rome to begin priestly formation because no seminary in the United States would accept him because of his race, but Tolton did so knowing that he might never return home again. This former slave's resolve to commit himself to priestly service meant that he literally would be forced to forsake home and family and move to Africa as a missionary. Recognizing, however, the faults in American society, the cardinal in charge of Tolton's seminary in Rome decided to send the first black priest from the United States back home. His argument? "America has been called the most enlightened nation; we will see if it deserves this honor."[6]

Several of the priests Tolton encountered at home in Quincy, Illinois, were not among the enlightened Americans, however, and they ended up running him out of town. Tolton never spoke ill of those who hurt him so viciously, but he was anxious to move to Chicago so that he could be free to exercise his ministry in a less racist location. Tolton took refuge in the Windy City, under

---

[6] Caroline Hemesath, *From Slave to Priest* (San Francisco: Ignatius Press, 2006), p. 154.

the patronage of Archbishop Patrick Feehan, where he worked to form a parish for local black Catholics. Tolton died at forty-three in 1897, an early death no doubt hastened by the many challenges he faced. The late Cardinal Francis E. George, O.M.I.—who regarded opening Tolton's cause for canonization as one of the most important ecclesiastical actions of his tenure as archbishop of Chicago—once said, "The Church is where you go when you want to be free."[7] Tolton's life was a living embodiment of this truth.

Henriette DeLille's life echoed this as well. Her perseverance, amid experiences similar to Tolton's, is astonishing and makes her witness important for our consideration today. And her difficulties within the Church were experienced after the difficulties in her own personal life, in a society that cheapened marriage and celebrated irregular families. Women of mixed race at DeLille's time in New Orleans—often descendants of slaves, as was DeLille—were often expected to form liaison relationships with white European men. They were expected to bear and rear their children, while being kept nearly as concubines. And, although their social status and living situation was more than comfortable, the abuse of their personhood was abominable. DeLille, like generations of her female forebears, lived according to this plaçage system. Yet it seems clear that DeLille longed for a more fulfilling life.

As she wrote in 1836, she longed "to live and die for God".[8] Having experienced an intensification in her call to discipleship, DeLille sought out religious life. But discriminatory rules enforced within the Church then made

[7] Francis Cardinal George, O.M.I., *A Godly Humanism: Clarifying the Hope that Lies Within* (Washington, D.C.: CUA Press, 2015), 75.

[8] Written by Henriette's hand on May 2, 1836, in a personal prayer book retained by the Sisters of the Holy Family in New Orleans.

things difficult for her, at least at first. As a woman of mixed race, no convent in New Orleans would allow her entry. Eventually, the local archbishop accepted her proposal to live as a consecrated woman, despite ecclesiastical officials' hesitancy that she appear publicly as one. In fact, the Sisters of the Holy Family, which DeLille founded, were unable to wear habits until years after DeLille's death in 1862. While some critics today choose to emphasize how DeLille should have never been forced to begin a new religious congregation—a correct assessment, by the way—focusing only on that portion of her story diminishes and trivializes the boldness, audacity, and character that underscored DeLille's pursuit of religious life. Her strength, courage, determination, and indomitability remain a model for all who hunger and thirst for righteousness.

Disciples in Mission

The most contemporary of the Holy Six, having died in her early fifties in 1990, was Sister Thea Bowman. As a writer, teacher, musician, and evangelist, Bowman preached the challenges to Gospel discipleship with clarity and zeal. Promoting ecclesial and cultural unity, Bowman used her prophetic voice to share the black Catholic experience. She knew that a Church divided or lacking in Christ's love could not be effective or credible in her mission.

This granddaughter of slaves exuded a love for the black Christian tradition, a truth that was on full display in her legendary 1989 address to the general assembly of U.S. bishops. As Bowman charged those present to join arms and lend their voices to hers in the spiritual "We Shall Overcome", her speech that day brought to the fore both the gifts and beauty of black Catholicism while effecting a rare and clear unity among the body of bishops.

While Bowman experienced prejudice and racism growing up, even in the convent, she was clear that love was the path forward, saying, "We must return love, no matter what."[9] Bowman's most formative years, influenced by the struggle for civil rights, helped her see the need not only to speak up, but to help bring healing where racism marred society, the culture, and the Church. In a 1987 interview, Bowman illustrated what the reality that a person of faith comes to realize when working for matters of principle: "I think the difference between me and some people is that I'm content to do my little bit. Sometimes people think they have to do big things in order to make change. But if each one would light a candle we'd have a tremendous light."[10]

The Path Ahead

The sin of racism has inflicted hatred and incited violence in every generation of American history, including our own. But as the lives of each of these six holy men and women show us, holiness is how God's children must respond to this sin. The stories of the righteous men and women of the Bible are often stark reminders of how God raises up and sustains witnesses to defend what God has revealed about the human person, to promote respect, harmony, and justice. Although many in the Church have not been consistent Gospel witnesses in the face of slavery and racial discrimination, each of the Holy Six teach us consistently and clearly

[9] Sister Thea Bowman, interview by Joe Smith, WMTV Madison, WI, 1988.
[10] Sister Thea Bowman, interview by Mike Wallace, *60 Minutes*, CBS, 1987.

how to love with Christ's heart in the face of hatred. While they experienced hardships, suffering, and animosity, they did not let themselves succumb to it or respond in kind. These men and women show us that we can overcome the sins that bind us and work together to bring healing and wholeness to humanity.

It is my hope that Catholics in the United States will come to recognize the greatest of humanity in the Holy Six. I hope that they become household names and that our children will know their stories. I hope that their causes of canonization will be promoted, supported, and encouraged. I hope that people will commend to them their most urgent and intimate needs for intercession. I hope that the Church will call them saints with speed and resolve. If we do not want our children and our children's children to repeat the sins of the past and present, we must see to it that these holy men and women occupy an important place in their imaginations and faith lives.

Sister Thea Bowman once said, "Maybe I'm not making big changes in the world. But if I have somehow helped or encouraged somebody along the journey, then I've done what I'm called to do."[11] Let us pray that this is true for each of us as we endeavor to become the saints God calls us to be. And may the Holy Six help us by their example and prayers.

[11] Sister Thea Bowman, quoted in *Wisdom Found: Stories of Women Transfigured by Faith*, ed. Lindsay Hardin Freeman (Cincinnati: Forward Movement Press, 2011), 25.

BIBLIOGRAPHY

Abbott, Walter M., S.J., ed. *The Documents of Vatican II.* New York: Corpus Books, 1967.

Anthony, Deacon Gerard-Marie. "Being Critical of Critical Race Theory". *Crisis Magazine*, May 10, 2021. https://www.crisismagazine.com/2021/being-critical-of-critical-race-theory.

Associated Press. "Black Catholics: Words Not Enough as Church Decries Racism". Voice of America, June 22, 2020. https://www.voanews.com/usa/race-america/black-catholics-words-not-enough-church-decries-racism.

Balmes, Jaime Luciano. *European Civilization: Protestantism and Catholicity Compared.* Translated by C.J. Hanford and Robert Kershaw. Baltimore: Murphy, 1850. Original Spanish edition: Jaime Luciano Balmes. *El Protestantismo Comparado Con El Catolicismo.* Barcelona: Brusi, 1849.

Bamberger, Abbot John Eudes. *The Abbey Psalter: The Book of Psalms Used by the Trappist Monks of Genesee Abbey.* Mahwah, N.J.: Paulist Press, 1981.

Bradley, Anthony B. *Liberating Black Theology: The Bible and the Black Experience in America.* Wheaton, Ill.: Crossway, 2010.

Braxton, Bishop Edward K. *The Church and the Racial Divide: Reflections of an African American Catholic Bishop.* Maryknoll, N.Y.: Orbis Books, 2021.

———. "The Horizon of Possibilities: 'The Catholic Church and the Racial Divide in the United States: Old Wounds Reopened'". Address given at the Catholic University of America, Washington, D.C., October 23, 2017. http://www.diobelle.org/our-bishop/writings/1133-the-horizon-of-possibilities-the-catholic-church-and-the-racial-divide-in-the-united-states-old-wounds-reopened.

Burke-Sivers, Deacon Harold. *Behold the Man: A Catholic Vision of Male Spirituality*. San Francisco: Ignatius Press, 2015.

———. *Father Augustus Tolton: The Slave Who Became the First African-American Priest*. Irondale, Ala.: EWTN Publishing, 2018.

Butcher, Jonathan, and Mike Gonzalez. "Critical Race Theory, the New Intolerance, and Its Grip on America". Heritage Foundation, December 7, 2020. https://www.heritage.org/civil-rights/report/critical-race-theory-the-new-intolerance-and-its-grip-america.

Catechism of the Catholic Church. 2nd ed. Washington, D.C.: Libreria Editrice Vaticana—United States Conference of Catholic Bishops, 1997. Updated 2016.

Catholic Online. "Black Racism in America Won't End Until Blacks Decide to End It—'Racism in America'". July 27, 2013. https://www.catholic.org/news/politics/story.php?id=51819.

Clay, Brandon, and Frost Smith. "Critical Race Theory in the Church". Answers in Genesis, September 29, 2020. https://answersingenesis.org/racism/critical-race-theory-church/.

Clement I. *Letter to the Corinthians* 35. Translated by John Keith. In *Ante-Nicene Fathers*, vol. 9. Edited by Allan Menzies. Buffalo, N.Y.: Christian Literature Publishing, 1896. Revised and edited for New Advent by Kevin Knight. http://www.newadvent.org/fathers/1010.htm.

CNA Staff. "Can Catholics Support 'Black Lives Matter'?" *Catholic World Report*, June 17, 2020. https://www.catholicworldreport.com/2020/06/17/can-catholics-support-black-lives-matter/.

Code of Canon Law, New English Translation. Washington, D.C.: Libreria Editrice Vaticana—Canon Law Society of America, 1989.

Cone, James H. *A Black Theology of Liberation*. New York: J.B. Lippincott, 1970.

———. *For My People: Black Theology and the Black Church*. Maryknoll, N.Y.: Orbis Books, 1996.

Congregation for Catholic Education. *"Male and Female He Created Them": Towards a Path of Dialogue on the Question of Gender Theory in Education*, February 2, 2019. https://www.vatican.va/roman_curia/congregations/ccatheduc/documents/rc_con_ccatheduc_doc_20190202_maschio-e-femmina_en.pdf.

Congregation for Divine Worship and the Discipline of the Sacraments. Instruction: Inculturation and the Roman Liturgy, March 29, 1994. https://www.ewtn.com/catholicism/library/instruction-inculturation-and-the-roman-liturgy-2180.

Congregation for the Doctrine of the Faith. Instruction on Certain Aspects of the "Theology of Liberation", August 6, 1984. https://www.vatican.va/roman_curia/congregations/cfaith/documents/rc_con_cfaith_doc_19840806_theology-liberation_en.html.

―――. Instruction on Certain Bioethical Questions *Dignitas Personae*, September 8, 2008. https://www.vatican.va/roman_curia/congregations/cfaith/documents/rc_con_cfaith_doc_20081208_dignitas-personae_en.html.

Copeland, M. Shawn, ed. *Uncommon Faithfulness: The Black Catholic Experience.* Maryknoll, N.Y.: Orbis Books, 2009.

Davis, Cyprian, O.S.B. *The History of Black Catholics in the United States.* New York: Crossroad Publishing, 1990.

Davis, Cyprian, O.S.B., and Diana L. Hayes, eds. *Taking Down Our Harps: Black Catholics in the United States.* Maryknoll, N.Y.: Orbis Books, 1998.

Davis, Cyprian, O.S.B., and Jamie T. Phelps, O.P., eds. *"Stamped with the Image of God": African Americans as God's Image in Black.* Maryknoll, N.Y.: Orbis Books, 2003.

Delgado, Richard, and Jean Stefancic. *Critical Race Theory: An Introduction.* 3rd ed. New York: New York University Press, 2017.

Derosa, John. "Does the Bible Support Slavery?" *Catholic Answers*, July 6, 2020. https://www.catholic.com/magazine/online-edition/does-the-bible-support-slavery.

Diamond, James A. "The Treatment of Non-Israelite Slaves: From Moses to Moses". TheTorah.com, 2022. https://www.thetorah.com/article/the-treatment-of-non-israelite-slaves-from-moses-to-moses.

Dunn, James D. G. *The Theology of Paul the Apostle*. Grand Rapids, Mich.: Eerdmans, 2006.

Gakunzi, David. "The Arab-Muslim Slave Trade: Lifting the Taboo". *Jewish Political Studies Review* 29, nos. 3–4 (September 3, 2018). https://jcpa.org/article/the-arab-muslim-slave-trade-lifting-the-taboo/.

Grant, George. *Grand Illusions: The Legacy of Planned Parenthood*. 2nd ed. Franklin, Tenn.: Adroit Press, 1992.

Gutiérrez, Gustavo. "Notes for a Theology of Liberation". *Theological Studies* 31, no. 2 (May 1970): 243–61.

Ha, Taylor. "Catholic Scholars Confront Racism and Describe How Fellow Catholics Can Help". Fordham News, June 9, 2020. https://news.fordham.edu/living-the-mission/catholic-scholars-confront-racism-and-describe-how-fellow-catholics-can-help/.

Harris, Sam, and William Lane Craig. "The God Debate", April 12, 2011. Center for Philosophy of Religion, University of Notre Dame, Notre Dame, Ind. Video, 33:14–39:01. https://www.youtube.com/watch?v=oAv_A-zJz1I.

Hauf, John, ed. *The Message of Fatima: Lucia Speaks*. Washington, N.J.: AMI Press, 1997.

Heinlein, Michael R., ed. *Black Catholics on the Road to Sainthood*. Huntington, Ind.: Our Sunday Visitor, 2021.

Hoopes, Tom. "Only the Church Does Anti-Racism Right". *National Catholic Register*, January 18, 2021. https://www.ncregister.com/commentaries/anti-racism-tolton.

Horn, Trent. "Slavery and the New Testament". *Catholic Answers*, September 1, 2016. https://www.catholic.com/magazine/print-edition/slavery-and-the-new-testament.

Howze, Joseph L., et al. *"What We Have Seen and Heard": A Pastoral Letter on Evangelization from the Black Bishops of the United States*. Cincinnati: St. Anthony Messenger Press, 1984. https://www.usccb.org/issues-and-action/cultural-diversity/african-american/resources/upload/what-we-have-seen-and-heard.pdf.

Hymowitz, Kay S., "The Black Family: 40 Years of Lies". *City Journal*. Summer 2005. https://www.city-journal.org/html/black-family-40-years-lies-12872.html.

Ignatius Catholic Study Bible: The New Testament; Revised Standard Version, Second Catholic Edition. Edited by Scott Hahn and Curtis Mitch. San Francisco: Ignatius Press, 2010.

International Theological Commission. *Communion and Stewardship: Human Persons Created in the Image of God,* July 23, 2004. https://www.vatican.va/roman_curia/congrega tions/cfaith/cti_documents/rc_con_cfaith_doc_20040723 _communion-stewardship_en.html.

Jennings, Willie James. *The Christian Imagination: Theology and the Origins of Race.* New Haven: Yale University Press, 2010.

John Paul II. Apostolic Exhortation on the Role of the Christian Family in the Modern World *Familiaris Consortio,* November 22, 1981. https://www.vatican.va/content /john-paul-ii/en/apost_exhortations/documents/hf_jp -ii_exh_19811122_familiaris-consortio.html.

———. Apostolic letter *Mulieris Dignitatem,* August 15, 1988. https://www.vatican.va/content/john-paul-ii/en/apost _letters/1988/documents/hf_jp-ii_apl_19880815_mulieris -dignitatem.html.

———. Apostolic letter *Salvifici Doloris,* February 11, 1984. https://www.vatican.va/content/john-paul-ii/en/apost _letters/1984/documents/hf_jp-ii_apl_11021984_salvifici -doloris.html.

———. Encyclical letter *Dives in Misericordia* (Rich in Mercy), November 30, 1980. https://www.vatican.va/content /john-paul-ii/en/encyclicals/documents/hf_jp-ii_enc _30111980_dives-in-misericordia.html#-27.

———. Encyclical letter *Evangelium Vitae* (Gospel of Life), March 25, 1995. https://www.vatican.va/content/john-paul-ii/en /encyclicals/documents/hf_jp-ii_enc_25031995_evange lium-vitae.html.

———. Encyclical letter *Veritatis Splendor* (The Splendor of Truth), August 6, 1993. https://www.vatican.va/content /john-paul-ii/en/encyclicals/documents/hf_jp-ii_enc _06081993_veritatis-splendor.html.

———. "Meaning of Man's Original Solitude, General Audience of October 10, 1979". Taken from *L'Osservatore Romano,* weekly edition in English, October 15, 1979,

14. https://www.ewtn.com/catholicism/library/meaning-of-mans-original-solitude-8510.

————. Meeting with the Black Catholic Community of New Orleans, September 12, 1987. https://www.vatican.va/content/john-paul-ii/en/speeches/1987/september/documents/hf_jp-ii_spe_19870912_cattolici-new-orleans.html.

————. Post-Synodal Apostolic Exhortation on Reconciliation and Penance *Reconciliatio et Paenitentia*, December 2, 1984. https://www.vatican.va/content/john-paul-ii/en/apost_exhortations/documents/hf_jp-ii_exh_0212 1984_reconciliatio-et-paenitentia.html.

Johnson, Andre E. "Where Did White Evangelicalism's Hatred of Critical Race Theory Really Begin?" Religion Dispatches, June 23, 2021. https://religiondispatches.org/where-did-white-evangelicalisms-hatred-of-critical-race-theory-really-begin/.

King, Martin Luther, Jr. "Acceptance Speech". University of Oslo, Oslo, Norway, December 10, 1964. NobelPrize.org. https://www.nobelprize.org/prizes/peace/1964/king/acceptance-speech/.

————. "Letter from Birmingham Jail", April 16, 1963. https://letterfromjail.com/.

————. *The Measure of a Man*. Philadelphia: Christian Education Press, 1959.

"Kingdom Race Theology #1—Sermon by Dr. Tony Evans". Oak Cliff Bible Fellowship, July 14, 2021. Video, 13:50–16:21, posted August 2, 2021. https://www.youtube.com/watch?v=ao7sNItCkAY.

Kirsch, Adam. "The Godfather of Critical Race Theory". *Wall Street Journal*, June 25, 2021. https://www.wsj.com/articles/the-godfather-of-critical-race-theory-11624627522.

Lowcountry Digital History Initiative. "Pope Nicolas V and the Portuguese Slave Trade". Lowcountry Digital Library, College of Charleston. Accessed December 15, 2022. http://ldhi.library.cofc.edu/exhibits/show/african_laborers_for_a_new_emp/pope_nicolas_v_and_the_portugu.

————. "Slavery before the Trans-Atlantic Trade". Lowcountry Digital Library, College of Charleston. Accessed December 13, 2021. http://ldhi.library.cofc.edu/exhibits/show /africanpassageslowcountryadapt/introductionatlanticworld /slaverybeforetrade.

Lucey, Candice. "How Did Different Races Come into Existence as God's Wonderful Created Image?" Christianity. com, June 15, 2020. https://www.christianity.com/wiki /bible/how-did-different-races-come-into-existence-as -gods-wonderful-created-image.html.

MAAFA 21: Black Genocide in the 21st Century. Denton, Tex.: Life Dynamics, 2009. DVD.

Marx, Karl, and Friedrich Engels. *Manifesto of the Communist Party.* In Selected Works, 1:98–137. Moscow: Progress Publishers, 1969. https://www.marxists.org/archive/marx /works/1848/communist-manifesto/index.htm.

Massingale, Bryan N. *Racial Justice and the Catholic Church.* Maryknoll, N.Y.: Orbis Books, 2010.

Morabito, Stella. "Critical Race Theory Is a Classic Communist Divide-and-Conquer Tactic". *Federalist,* September 29, 2020. https://thefederalist.com/2020/09/29/critical-race-theory-is-a-classic-communist-divide-and-conquer-tactic/.

National Black Catholic Congress XII. *Pastoral Plan of Action,* November 27, 2017. https://nbccongress.org/wp-content /uploads/2021/10/Congress-12-Patrola-Plan.pdf.

National Conference of Catholic Bishops. *Brothers and Sisters to Us: U.S. Catholic Bishops' Pastoral Letter on Racism.* Washington, D.C.: United States Catholic Conference, 1979. https://www.usccb.org/committees/african-american -affairs/brothers-and-sisters-us.

National Conference of Catholic Bishops. Committee on African American Catholics. *Love Thy Neighbor As Thyself: U.S. Catholic Bishops Speak against Racism; January 1997– June 2000.* Washington, D.C.: United States Catholic Conference, 2001.

National Conference of Catholic Bishops. Committee on African American Catholics. *Keep Your Hand on the Plow: The*

African American Presence in the Catholic Church. Washington, D.C.: United States Catholic Conference, 1996.

Osterman, Michelle J.K., et al. "Births: Final Data for 2020". *National Vital Statistics Reports* 70, no. 17 (February 7, 2022). https://www.cdc.gov/nchs/data/nvsr/nvsr70/nvsr70-17.pdf.

Panzer, Joel S. *The Popes and Slavery.* New York: Alba House, 1996.

Paul VI. Apostolic letter *Octogesima Adveniens*, May 14, 1971. https://www.vatican.va/content/paul-vi/en/apost_letters/documents/hf_p-vi_apl_19710514_octogesima-adveniens.html.

―――. Encyclical Letter on the Regulation of Birth *Humane Vitae*, July 25, 1968. https://www.vatican.va/content/paul-vi/en/encyclicals/documents/hf_p-vi_enc_25071968_humanae-vitae.html.

Peffer, R.G. *Marxism, Morality, and Social Justice.* Princeton, N.J.: Princeton University Press, 1990.

Phelps, Jamie T., O.P., ed. *Black and Catholic: The Challenge and Gift of Black Folk—Contributions of African American Experience and Thought to Catholic Theology.* 2nd ed. Milwaukee: Marquette University Press, 2002.

Pokorsky, Jerry J. "Racism and Catholicism". *Catholic Thing,* September 2, 2017. https://www.thecatholicthing.org/2017/09/02/racism-and-catholicism/.

Pontifical Commission for Justice and Peace. *The Church and Racism: Towards a More Fraternal Society,* November 3, 1988. https://www.ewtn.com/catholicism/library/church-and-racism-towards-a-more-fraternal-society-2426.

Pontifical Council for Justice and Peace. *Compendium of the Social Doctrine of the Church,* April 2, 2004. https://www.vatican.va/roman_curia/pontifical_councils/justpeace/documents/rc_pc_justpeace_doc_20060526_compendio-dott-soc_en.html.

Pope, Monsignor Charles. "Not Peace but the Sword". *Community in Mission* (blog). Archdiocese of Washington, July 12, 2020. https://blog.adw.org/2020/07/not-peace-but-the-sword/.

———. "What Was the Lord Doing on Monday of Holy Week?" *Community in Mission* (blog). Archdiocese of Washington, March 29, 2021. https://blog.adw.org/2021/03/what-was-the-lord-doing-on-monday-of-holy-week/.

Pritchard, James B., ed. *Ancient Near Eastern Texts Relating to the Old Testament*. Princeton, N.J.: Princeton University Press, 1969.

Purvis, Gloria. "What Will It Take to Respect Life in the Black Community?" Lecture, National Black Catholic Convocation I, Indianapolis, Ind., April 21, 2004.

Segura, Olga M. *Birth of a Movement: Black Lives Matter and the Catholic Church*. Maryknoll, N.Y.: Orbis Books, 2021.

Sontag, Frederick. "Liberation Theology and Its View of Political Violence". *Journal of Church and State* 31, no. 2 (1989): 269–86. http://www.jstor.org/stable/23916796.

Sowell, Thomas. *Marxism: Philosophy and Economics*. New York: Quill, 1985.

United States Conference of Catholic Bishops. Committee on Cultural Diversity in the Church. *Open Wide Our Hearts: The Enduring Call to Love; A Pastoral Letter against Racism*. Washington, D.C.: United States Conference of Catholic Bishops, 2018. https://www.usccb.org/issues-and-action/human-life-and-dignity/racism/upload/open-wide-our-hearts.pdf.

Vatican Council II. Dogmatic Constitution on the Church *Lumen Gentium*, November 21, 1964. https://www.vatican.va/archive/hist_councils/ii_vatican_council/documents/vat-ii_const_19641121_lumen-gentium_en.html.

———. Dogmatic Constitution on Divine Revelation *Dei Verbum*, November 18, 1965. https://www.vatican.va/archive/hist_councils/ii_vatican_council/documents/vat-ii_const_19651118_dei-verbum_en.html.

———. Pastoral Constitution on the Church in the Modern World *Gaudium et Spes*, December 7, 1965. https://www.vatican.va/archive/hist_councils/ii_vatican_council/documents/vat-ii_const_19651207_gaudium-et-spes_en.html.

Von Balthasar, Hans Urs. *You Crown the Year with Your Goodness: Sermons through the Liturgical Year.* San Francisco: Ignatius Press, 1989.

Wetter, Gustav A. *Dialectical Materialism.* Westport, Conn.: Greenwood Press, 1977.

White, Matthew. "The Black Chapter of Communism". In *The Great Big Book of Horrible Things: The Definitive Chronicle of History's 100 Worst Atrocities.* New York: W. W. Norton, 2011.

Williams, Shannen Dee. "Racism Has Always Been a Pro-Life Issue". CatholicPhilly.com, June 12, 2020. https://catholicphilly.com/2020/06/commentaries/racism-has-always-been-a-pro-life-issue/.

Winfield, Nicole, and Elana Schor. "Pope Sends Strong Message to US Catholics after Floyd Death". AP News, June 10, 2020. https://apnews.com/article/donald-trump-us-news-ap-top-news-international-news-police-10a84cc07 3faf4786f1c252e6bdf6a42.

Wright, Will. "Racism: A Catholic Response". Catholic-Link.com. Accessed January 10, 2023. https://catholic-link.org/racism-a-catholic-response/.

Xu, Kenny. "Critical Race Theory's Poisonous Roots Trace Back to Harvard University". *Federalist*, June 9, 2021. https://thefederalist.com/2021/06/09/critical-race-theorys-poisonous-roots-trace-back-to-harvard-university/.

INDEX

SCRIPTURAL INDEX